Winning Pare

Winning Child

Parenting so that everybody wins

Jan Fortune-Wood

Cinnamon Press

Books that are the spice of life

Published by Cinnamon Press
Meirion House, Glan yr afon, Tanygrisiau,
Blaenau Ffestiniog, Gwynedd, LL41 3SU
www.cinnamonpress.com

First published in Great Britain in 2005

ISBN 978-0-9549433-0-1

British Library Cataloguing in Publication Data
A CIP record for this book can be obtained from the British Library

Designed and typeset in Arial by Cinnamon Press
Cover design by Mike Fortune-Wood

Printed in Great Britain by the MPG Books Group,
Bodmin and King's Lynn

Cinnamon Press

Meirion House, Glan yr afon, Tanygrisiau,

Blaenau Ffestiniog, Gwynedd, LL41 3SU

www.cinnamonpress.com

Acknowledgements

The people who have contributed to my thinking or have offered practical and moral support during the writing of this book are many more than I can name.

I particularly owe a great deal of thanks to Roland and Janet Meighan of Educational Heretics Press, who gave me the space and freedom to develop my thinking in earlier manuscripts; to Sarah Fitz-Claridge for her inspiration; to Andy Blewett and everyone who has attended my workshops in Dorset over the last five years and to all the families I've worked with in person, at conferences or online.

Very special thanks are due to Stella Howden and Sue Cvach, who offered valuable feedback and criticism of the manuscript as well as invaluable encouragement and support.

Most of all thank you to my family; who are my reason for wanting to learn more about how to live so that everyone wins.

vi

Introduction:
Parenting so that everybody wins?

This book is not like most parenting books you will read. In parenting, as in any other arena of life, everyone wants to win. Parents want to win, children want to win and what usually ensues is anything from a battle to an uneasy compromise, but it doesn't have to be that way. There is no magic way of changing things, but there is a way: clear your mind, suspend disbelief and imagine an environment where adults and children alike are winners. This book is not about getting children to do what you want. On the contrary, I am actually suggesting that children should get what they want. On the other hand, I'm also suggesting that this will not result in spoiled brats who will exhaust you with their demands, rob you of any life of your own and then want more. Far from it! Helping your children to get what they want in life should not be the opposite of you, the parent, getting what you want out of life too. We can all live together well in ways that parents and children consent to and enjoy.

What parent hasn't longed to improve his or her relationship with children? What parent hasn't thought to herself 'Surely, there must be a better way than this', but felt defeated and trapped by old ways of relating? This book is about that better way. It's not magic; relationships are demanding, complex things, but imagine that all of the energy you've ever used on fighting your children, cajoling your children, begging your children, compelling your children, even hurting your children, could go instead into finding solutions with them; solutions that they want, solutions that you want; solutions in which everyone is a winner.

The parenting ideas that you are about to consider propose that in place of compulsion we can find mutual solutions with children, in other words win-win situations that respect children, and assist them to grow as independent people. In this book I want us to consider the idea that when we use compulsion on another human being we risk damaging that person's ability to think clearly. Moreover, people who can't think clearly are cut off from their personal wishes and motivations; from all that makes them the unique individuals they are.

Like any book about relationships, this book makes some assumptions and the most basic assumption of this book is that people are not born irrational. Rather we begin life as resourceful beings with reasoning brains, instincts for self preservation and personal driving forces that are healthy. If we assume this, then it is reasonable to think that if children are given information, encouraged to learn through making guesses about the world and finding out which guesses fit and which fail, then they will develop and flourish. On the other hand, when children's experiments are interrupted by force, however subtle, a line of thought is sabotaged in its tracks. In such cases, children are left in a state of turmoil with the painful feeling of being thwarted.

Parenting is an enormous undertaking. The last thing parents need is to be judged or made to feel guilty for every little error they make with their children. None of us wants to be put on the defensive, feeling that we have to justify every action against some impossible, perfect standard of ideal parenting. We all make mistakes, but we can improve on them. We can build relationships in which mutual problem solving, optimism and improvement dominate. Consent based parenting is about doing our limited best now, while learning all the time. We can all get our own way, parents and children alike, and be better people for it. How? That's what this book will seek to answer.

Part 1:
A World of Consent

Most of us want parenting advice that is practical, and this book aims to give that, but trying to find another way of parenting also demands that we do a bit of thinking. The way we think about our children and our relationship to them; the way we speak to and about our children, make all the difference to the way we act. To begin to find consent with our children we have to ask some previously unasked questions and take apart thoughts that we once thought were obvious or common sense.

In the first part of the book I want to introduce you to the world of consent. Firstly, I want to explore what is meant by assisting children to be free people. When I first encountered such ideas my hackles were raised; liberal I might be, but insanely negligent I was not. I thought, "So what should a parent do? Let her four year old play on the motorway because he wants to while her six year old daughter watches porn films?" I had seriously misunderstood both the idea and the practice of living by consent. A child getting what he wants is not about neglect; it doesn't mean never making suggestions, never offering alternatives, never encouraging children to change their minds. On the other hand, neither is finding agreement with children simply a ruse to get children to do what we want without having to force and cajole and fight.

Eventually, the penny dropped: compulsion really is damaging and it has to go, it is simply not the innocent parenting tool that I had always imagined it to be, no matter how subtly employed; but without this last line of defense what was I supposed to do? I needed new ideas. I needed to think again about my role as parent. I needed to think through issues of safety, protection, neglect, self-surrender and giving in as a parent. Those are the issues I'll address in chapters one and two.

For a while all went well; it was like cracking a code or buying a new pair of spectacles that make everything clear again. My thinking changed, my speech changed, my relationships changed. Unfortunately though, parents never arrive at the final destination; this is a lifetime's process of improvement, not a simple, soluble puzzle. I soon found myself hard up against deeply ingrained ideas that stopped me finding solutions and left me feeling trapped and frustrated. Why? Well, we all have our own areas in which our thinking is poor or less worked out and we all have some ideas that run so deep that we find them hard even to notice, let alone criticize and change.

So, in chapter three I want to look more closely at the obstacles in our way; the ideas that prevent us from living by consent. These things are very personal. Most conventional parents agree that there are certain things that require compulsion, yet no one agrees what those things are. Perhaps you have no hang ups about bed times, room tidiness, watching TV and eating sweets, but feel that the world will end if teeth are not brushed twice a day, so you are prepared to compel your child to brush her teeth if you can't convince her?

These deeply rooted ideas, which are often less than rational in the way they are thought about and expressed, rely on what the scientist Richard Dawkins calls 'memes'. Memes are ideas that reproduce themselves in much the same way as genes reproduce themselves in the biological realm. In chapter three I want to explore with you the idea of memes (no scientific knowledge needed!); what they mean for our parenting, how they might affect us and how we can change our thinking when it places obstacles in the path to living by consent. Living by consent is not a set of techniques; it is about creating a lively, problem-solving environment in which everyone is on the same side in the journey.

1

Helping Children, Helping Ourselves

How is it possible to live family life without compromise? How can we always have win-win situations? How can responsible parents let go of the notion of having clear and safe rules for their children? First, we have to think that it is possible; we have to be optimists above all else.

In the film, The Matrix, the central character, Neo, discovers that he has been living in a world that is constructed for him, inside a fake reality that is designed to maximize the external controls imposed by the rulers. He also discovers that he can choose not to accept this version of reality. He is offered the opportunity to find out the truth of what the world is really like by making a choice between two pills. The blue pill will wipe out his memory of ever having doubts about the world as he sees it. The red pill will show him the truth, but life will never be the same again. Everything that he had previously thought to be the case will be transformed and challenged. Neo takes the red pill. Embarking on finding another way to parent is like taking that red pill; everything will change; you will question everything. It's unnerving, but it's a great adventure.

Consent based parenting is just as exciting as Neo's choice. We can choose to live in ways that don't rely on rules or conflict between parents and children, but we need to know how to start. The place to start is in your head.

Become an Optimistic Parent

Once we think something is impossible we are generally on a hiding to nowhere. Optimism actually makes a difference. If we are genuinely going to help our children get what they want from life and enjoy life ourselves then we need to be optimistic parents who have dealt with some fears and doubts. So I want to look at some of the doubts that might already be taking shape in your thoughts and, in the process, help you to find the confidence to go on asking the questions with the simple aim of helping you to help your children.

To become this optimistic parent we first have to dispel a few myths. Some notions seem obvious, but actually are deeply questionable. To become an optimistic parent we have to think that compulsion isn't our friend and instead develop new ideas.

Compulsion isn't our friend

We are quite used to the idea that sometimes children have to be made to do things. It is a very rare parent who enjoys forcing a child to do anything, but by and large the view is that a bit of compulsion is harmless or sometimes just the lesser evil. Of course most people also think that certain acts of force are obviously wrong; it's not uncommon to frown on beating a child, but accept that a tap on the hand to prevent a toddler from touching a fire is justified. Most of us draw a line that we wouldn't cross; we might not agree with any kind of physical discipline, but a stiff talking to, being grounded or losing pocket money might seem to be useful ways of motivating good and responsible behavior.

Most of us think that compulsion is inevitable. Such acts of force, we tell ourselves, are the normal stuff of life that all of us have to be able to accept and get over quickly. Well, they are certainly commonplace, but I want you to think again; not so that you can wallow in guilt, but simply so that you can live differently.

Meet Alex, a lively four-year-old who has been brought up in a caring, busy family. He has an older sister, Jenny, who is seven and a baby brother, Jack. His Dad works long hours, sometimes away from home overnight, and his Mum, Emma, is beginning to feel over tired. Baby Jack likes to do some of his feeding at night, but tends to have a long sleep in the evening from around eight o'clock. Jenny, tired out by school, happily settles down by eight in the evening and Emma thinks this would be an ideal time to get some extra sleep for herself, especially on those evenings when her partner, Steve, is away from home. The problem is Alex. Alex has never seemed to need a great deal of sleep. He's only recently begun to sleep through the night, but he simply won't settle down as early as eight in the evening. To make matters worse, he also wants to be up early in the morning. Emma is at the end of her tether, she is worn out and often feels bad tempered and resentful with Alex during the daytime.

Emma reads parenting books and consults her friends, convinced that it is Alex's intransigence that is causing her all these problems. Everything would be much better for everyone, Alex included, if she could go to bed early two or three times a week. Everyone tells her that she has to get tough with Alex, for his sake and her own, and teach him that he has to go to bed at a 'reasonable' hour and stay there until a 'reasonable' hour.

We can all sympathize with Emma; being at home with young children, doing the lion's share of childcare and feeling sleep deprived into the bargain are not made any easier by being commonplace. Of course Emma needs more sleep. The mistake that conventional parenting theories, friends and Emma are making is to decide in advance that there is one solution and that this solution is so important that it is worth compelling Alex; even believing that the compulsion is as much for Alex's benefit as anyone else's. Later on, I'll return to the subject of finding solutions in tight corners like this one, but for now I want to concentrate not on the many possible solutions to this situation, but on Alex and the damage that may be being done to him.

We have to admit that we don't actually know what the damage is. The problem with using force, whether physical or emotional, is that it affects every individual in unique ways. Some children are seemingly impervious to what might look like horrific and substantial force. Other children can be put into states of turmoil from what seem to be very minor and everyday acts of subtle manipulation. One child triumphantly proclaims 'That didn't hurt!' as she is smacked for the tenth time that day, while another whimpers at the slightest cross look from his mother. It's for this reason that we can't establish an acceptable quota of force or manipulation that can be safely used on children. It's similar to a pregnant woman drinking alcohol. In theory there is no safe amount. That doesn't mean that one glass of champagne at your best friend's wedding is definitely going to harm your baby. It is simply that we can't actually know whether some miniscule or slightly larger damage might occur for that particular fetus at that particular stage of development or whether there will be no effect at all.

The effect of compulsion is something that happens in the mind of another human being, so when we talk about damage we are not talking about something measurable. We can't predict that one smack will result in 2% psychological damage or that six months of being forced to go to bed at a particular time will result in 4% psychological damage. Humans are simply not that predictable. What we can say is that every act of compulsion risks doing some damage to how that person thinks and to the child-parent relationship; trust is replaced with conflict and hurt.

Life is full of things to blame; if our children behave badly or grow up as unhappy individuals we have a ready list of culprits to reach for: sugar, E numbers, food allergies, pollution, TV, computers, syndromes like ADHD or Asperger's, peer pressure, schools, the decline of the church, the breakdown of community, changing standards of discipline or a thousand and one other bogeys. Amongst so many competing pressures and when it is obvious that parents, for the most part, care passionately about their children, it seems cruel and unhelpful to blame parents for their thirty-year-old son's sleep problems simply because they insisted on a certain bedtime when he was four. This book is not a charter for blame or guilt and nor am I attempting to make parents responsible for every little action of every child aged 0-90. What I do want to do is to help parents to re-think how they might live better lives with their children in this moment. We have all made mistakes in the past and we will all make mistakes in the future, but that doesn't need to stop us doing all that we humanly can to find optimistic and creative ways to do less harm and more good. If we look at compulsion differently and see force as potentially damaging then we will find other ways to live together well.

Ideas for the optimistic parent

To begin to rid ourselves of the idea that compulsion is a useful parenting tool, we need some new ideas to put in its place. When we talk about helping our children to help themselves we're talking about some new parenting ideas such as:

- swapping consent for compulsion
- treating children as reasonable people
- trusting our children and their built in desires
- recognizing our human limitations
- using the resourcefulness we all have
- believing that it is good to change our minds
- questioning the things we always assumed
- finding solutions that everyone wants
- being confident that solutions exist

These few simple ideas are the tools with which we can revolutionize family relationships.

Swapping consent for compulsion

One of the difficulties that parents new to this kind of parenting often have is that in the rush to drop compulsion they run into all kinds of tight corners. This can be demotivating and exhausting. The constant elimination of compulsion and manipulation from family life is necessary, but it is much more important to build systems of consent than to merely avoid force and compulsion. One way is to stop thinking of parents as authority figures and stop seeing children as sub-human, irrational beings.

If I have to find a solution with my adult friend then I have to do so without believing that I have authority over him or imaging that he is not capable of reasoning with me. The same is true with our children. Once we begin to think like this then avoiding compulsion becomes secondary to building consent, a much more positive way of living for everyone.

That said, we do need to have our antenna attuned for signs of compulsion. In this book I will use 'compulsion' to refer to any kind of constraint that is used to force a child to follow a course of behavior against her wishes. A child washing up whilst she really wants to climb a tree, a child who is made to put on a track suit to go shopping when he wants to go in his pajamas, or a child doing homework when she really wants to be watching her favorite TV show, would be obvious examples. Compulsion, though, is not always obvious. Perhaps the child working through a science workbook has been told by her parents to clean the rabbit hutch. The child wants to watch *The Simpsons*, but the parent is adamant that the hutch needs cleaning now, so the child responds that she was planning to get on with her science homework. The parent approves of this and agrees that this is a more worthwhile activity, at least for the time being. In the parent's hierarchy of activities, cleaning rabbit hutches shouldn't interrupt science homework any more than TV watching should interrupt pet care. The child is compelled against her will, even though she suggested doing the homework. How can she think clearly about these things when her mind is so full of tangled subterfuge?

Compulsion can be direct or it can be subtle and manipulative. Children want their parent's love and approval. Whenever love and approval are conditional, whether the condition is getting a high score in a spelling test, eating cabbage, or only watching parentally condoned television shows, there is compulsion. Anything that is done against the child's will, anything that causes the child to do or think one thing while he still wants to do or think something else, is compulsion.

That's not to say that we will always succeed in avoiding compulsion, but when we stop thinking of it as a fall back position, then we are much more likely to find other solutions. Children cannot trust that they have moved into a consensual environment or that it is in their interests to join in with the process of finding solutions if they know that the bottom line is that the parent reserves the right to compel. Children need to be confident that they don't have to come up with a solution that fits into the parental notion of necessary action if we want them to be secure enough to sometimes change their minds about what they want.

So what does consent mean?

- Children not being forced to follow one course of behavior whilst they wish to be doing something else.
- Children not being forced to resort to subterfuge in order to avoid certain acts of compulsion.

- Parents avoiding doing things that compel a child to act against his wishes, whether overtly or through a skillful repertoire of disapproving glances, sighs and postures that our children understand all too well.
- Parents not reserving compulsion as a last line of defense.

Consent based parenting is only going to work if your children can trust that your advice is your best idea, not just a backdoor method of control. Of course you'll make mistakes, and you can apologize, but apology is very different from justifying compulsion.

Treating children as reasonable people

When we talk about thinking damage caused by compulsion, we're not talking about the bruises an abused child receives in a violent home, but about something that takes place in the mind of the child. Force has the potential to affect how we think about things. The turmoil of having to do something whilst another wish is uppermost affects how Tom thinks. This is where reason comes in. Like adults, when children have the space to genuinely engage in a search for solutions they learn how to remain reasonable people.

There is often a tendency to believe that reasoning is something that develops with maturity and experience, and that it is dependent on our ability to construct an articulate argument. This kind of thinking allows that we can 'reason' with older children, but not with babies, toddlers and young children who are pre-verbal or have more limited articulacy and logic. In this book when I talk about reason and reasoning I don't mean having a certain level of articulacy, intellectual development or verbal logic. A baby knows what she needs and constantly creates new knowledge; as such she is reasonable. We can find solutions with any reasoning being. We may not always use words. We may sometimes use very simple words with visual and practical demonstration, but we will definitely be aware of a baby or toddler's wishes. We can also clearly see that toddlers and babies are able to move to new wishes or (in their own way) suggest new solutions to adults.

Children, like adults, are reasoning human beings. Of course that doesn't mean that a child will never act irrationally, any more than you or I will never act irrationally. However just because a child appears unreasonable on some occasion is no justification for using compulsion; adding more damage is only liable to make a child more irrational in the longer term. Even more importantly, we always have to be cautious when we are judging someone else's rationality. It is impossible to look into another mind. Sometimes when we think that our child is being irrational it is quite possible that they actually have an idea which deserves consideration, but our own irrationality stops us from seeing it. Getting into psychological guessing games is futile. We do far better to simply engage with each idea resourcefully, without being dismissive.

Respecting that children are at least as reasonable as anyone else entails:

- engaging with each idea, even when its seems challenging
- being open enough to constantly re-examine our own ideas
- being prepared to change our minds
- being determined to find solutions to problems
- avoiding making guesses about what is in the minds of others so that we stop labeling certain ideas or behavior 'irrational' (yes, we might be right, but we can't know for certain and more compulsion won't help!)

Trusting our children and their built in desires

Who owns a child? Sadly, few people think that the answer is the child himself. I will return to this subject in more depth in chapter 5, but for now I want to simply set out the position that each of us owns ourselves, even if we are only a few minutes old.

There are those who see themselves as radical and liberal thinkers who still have problems with this idea. The supposedly libertarian writer Roderick T. Long, for example, has argued that the fact of coming into the world as dependent beings implies the duty of obedience in return for the parental obligation to provide care. The justification is that children,

> "lack the capacity to make rational decisions about their lives.... Consider the analogy of a person in a coma; we make medical decisions for such persons without their consent, because we assume they would consent if they were able to do so... I suggest that children may be considered as instances of diminished capacity; guardians act as agents for children, treating the children as they judge the children would consent to be treated if their faculties were fully developed."

I want to suggest that not having verbal articulacy is not the same as being irrational or comatose. The tiniest babies exhibit their own motives, will and ability to gain new knowledge; in short they have all that is needed to enable us to problem solve with them without having to stamp on their deepest and most basic drives and wishes. Certainly parents have a duty to help their children (as I will discuss at length in chapter 2) but there is no good reason why this help should have to come in the guise of thwarting children or treating them as no more rational than coma victims.

Parents are certainly well placed to offer information and moral advice that makes sense according to the age and development of an individual child; parents should always be engaged with their children and not neglectful. Certainly there are extreme cases when we have to assume that we would have the child's consent all things being equal (some medical emergencies don't allow for discussion; a child of two with no understanding of physics and no safety equipment deciding to jump from the thirteenth floor of a tower block to gain an experience of falling, would be examples where we simply have to act), but these are rare occasions, not standard interactions in parent-child relationships.

We don't gradually become human and it is a condition of being a full human being that each person is a full and free self. There is no justification for spending the first years of a child's life causing distress or gradually treating the child we have harmed as incrementally less incapacitated.

If children have reason and if compulsion damages thinking then we need to be working with that reason and building an environment of consent from the moment we become aware that it is possible. This entails putting children's inner desires for their lives first. We are all unique. Each of us has ideas that we work from, genes that we have inherited, dispositions, characters, motives and wishes. These are not fixed and unchangeable and it is our ability to change these things that enables us to be resourceful, flexible, problem solving people. That said, we exercise our freedom in so far as we act in accord with our own motives. Parents have an enormous role in shaping a child's motives, but ultimately a child belongs to herself and she is free only if she is not thwarted in acting accordance with her own identity. The foundation of a free life is simply what it says it is; the freedom to act as we want (and I'll explain later why that does not mean that our children will act like immoral monsters).

Children are learning the most, growing the most and harmed the least when:

- they are treated as full, free human beings, not as property
- when they are doing the things that are in tune with their own motives
- when they are having fun and doing what they want

If the thought of all that terrifies you, take a deep breath and keep reading; we are talking about reasonable, moral children and young people here, not self destructive and wantonly harmful terrors.

Recognizing our human limitations

One thing that greatly assists consensual living is for parents to recognize their own limitations. If we take seriously the possibility that we might be wrong then we are much less likely to attempt to compel our view onto another, even when we strongly believe that it is correct. This recognition is central to rational parenting with consent. Our ideas may well be right, but we can never know that as an absolute certainty. We should always be open to the possibility that the other person, even if she is a distressed two-year old, has a better idea.

No-one is infallible, no-one knows everything, no-one is without short-comings, foibles and hang-ups. You may be wrong, even when you are sure that you're right. Being tentative keeps the search for solutions open and is much more likely to lead to an outcome everyone wants.

Using the resourcefulness we all have

Another crucial element in finding consent-based solutions is simple resourcefulness; the kind of creative and innovative ability to change our ideas in favor of something better, something that helps. Consent based parents have to be resourceful and their children's resourcefulness is also important. It's about:

- finding solutions
- everyone, parents and children, being open to changing their minds
- thinking of new ideas (not in the sense of world shattering new hypotheses, but simply discovering new ideas which are useful and relevant to your family.)

Changing our minds is a good thing

Along the way reason and resourcefulness are aided by the ability of everyone in a family to review ideas. We might think about this as 'criticism', but criticism generally has had a bad, if undeserved press, and this is certainly not an invitation to disparage your child's arguments or to be dismissive. A feature of helping children to get what they want is to engage with their ideas, point out problems and make genuine contributions. When there is no compulsion on the child to accept your alternative ideas, then they tend to feel more relaxed about listening and giving your suggestions real consideration. Review requires that we share:

- the best ideas, opinions, morals, information and suggestions that we have available
- that we offer our ideas without compulsion
- that we remain open to the possibility that our suggestions and assumptions may be wrong

- that we don't keep repeating the same ideas ad nauseam and long after our children have asked us to desist

Questioning the things we've always assumed

We all hold deeply rooted ideas, from states of mind to genetic dispositions to articulated ideas. All of us have our own assumptions, ideas and theories, some of them consciously held, others more inarticulate, but deeply ingrained; ideas that we might refer to as intuition or tendencies of thought and behavior.

Let's consider Ellen. After a childhood filled with conventional compulsion, Ellen grows up and becomes a parent. She is convinced that children need to eat a very careful diet to keep them healthy. Ellen assumes that a diet that is sugar free, additive free and vegan is best. Her child has other ideas, and months, if not years, of conflict and misery follow while Ellen imposes her 'essential' food assumptions on her son. It may be that Ellen has some good and reasonable ideas about eating, but she has become incapable of thinking openly and reasonably about food. No amount of reason or counter argument is going to convince Ellen that her son's brain and health do not require this particular and strict diet. Ellen's friends offer other good ideas. Ellen can see that her friends' children do not appear to be suffering from malnutrition, lethargy or the bizarre behaviors that she feels a wider diet would lead to, but she still can't bring herself to let go of her enormous fear that without a controlled diet her child will suffer. Ellen's ideas are entrenched. Parenting is a practical activity; it involves actions, but those actions rely on our thinking; our ideas and assumptions matter.

Ellen's practice as a parent is completely controlled by food assumptions that she can't even begin to evaluate. All of us have areas where our thinking is far from clear. All of us hold some ideas that are so deeply entrenched that they present obstacles in our way, often without us ever realizing that this is the case. This is a theme to which we will return in detail in chapter 3, but for now we simply need to realize that our thinking matters; assumptions count:

- assumptions are anything from morals to opinions to tendencies
- assumptions can be very deeply entrenched, sometimes so deeply that we do not even articulate them; they are unquestioned.
- assumptions can change, especially when we engage them with reason whilst recognizing our limitations.

Finding solutions that everyone wants

A key feature of any family trying to live by consent is the practice of finding mutual solutions. This is simply any solution to any problem that all the participants agree to be preferable to either their original solutions or to anything else they have considered. A mutual solution implies a win-win situation in which everyone is pleased with the outcome. It is not a compromise in which one person wins whilst others give way, reluctantly or sadly or with the poor option that they will get their turn to win another time. Mutual solutions rely on genuine consent. They also rely on the ability of the participants to change their original wishes during the process of problem solving. This does not mean that original wishes are never followed. Sometimes the original wish of one person may turn out to be the mutual solution of all, but unless there is a basic willingness to change and explore new ideas then no mutual solution can be reached. To find solutions we have to use reason and resourcefulness. It also requires that we have the optimism to believe that solutions to problems do exist, even if we don't always find them.

Within families, we are not used to win-win scenarios with everyone on the same side. We are used to assuming that often, if not always, someone must lose; that compromise is about as good as it gets, and that conflict is inevitable. This is not a utopian book and I am not advocating an elite parenting theory for perfect people or for parents chronically addicted to sacrificing themselves to their monstrously demanding children. Yet I can tell you that mutual solutions work. They work in large and small families, poor and rich families, families from every cultural and ethnic background, families with and without adherence to particular faiths, families with one parent or two parents or gay parents or living in communities. Mutual solutions work wherever there is a fundamental trust that children are reasonable and resourceful; wherever there is the essential realism to admit that we are all limited and therefore need to proceed with open minds; wherever we are willing to devote our time, energy, and resources to consent, instead of to conflict and damage.

Mutual solutions also require another basic assumption. In order to enter into the process of finding mutual solutions with our children, we have to believe that a child getting 'what he wants' is not the opposite of being moral and caring about others. Children expressing their wishes are simply doing the right thing for themselves, which may very well be the thing that also has great benefits for others as well. Why should we think that, given respect and treated as full human beings, our children will choose evil? It is a fear that is false and which needs questioning at every turn (an issue to which we will return). Mutual solutions are the final essential ingredient of consent based parenting; parenting so that everyone wins.

When we talk about mutual solutions we mean:

- solutions that everyone really desires (not compromises)
- solutions that have the consent of all parties
- solutions that are found when everyone engages their reason and resourcefulness
- solutions that are found when those involved are willing to change their minds (though that doesn't meant that first suggestions never become mutual solutions)
- solutions that take seriously that everyone getting what they want is a good thing.

Being confident that solutions exist

All of this brings me back to optimism. When we feel confident and resourceful and believe that problems can be solved, life improves. I will return to this theme more fully in chapter 10, but we from the outset we need to believe that the world is one in which solutions exist (at least in theory, even if they sometimes escape us). If our view of the universe is essentially pessimistic; if we think some problems are incapable of solution (even in theory in the far off mists of time) then we are much more likely to give up seeking solutions when things become hard.

- as part of a positive approach we need to value both the solutions we find, and the whole process of problem solving
- solutions do exist, even if our limitations hamper us in finding them.

Moving on as an Optimistic Parent

Helping our children to get what they want demands a whole new relationship between parents and children. It is a radical departure from most of what we thought we knew about being parents. It raises many questions. Isn't it likely to lead to neglect? What if the child wants to engage in all sorts of dangerous or immoral behaviors? Surely parents end up as slaves to every childish whim with no time or energy to do what they want in their own lives?

Doing something new always brings fears, but all of these questions can be answered. Consent based parenting is not a recipe for neglect, immorality, social services intervention or burnt out parents; feel the fear and live well anyway. Life will never be the same again and, once you have begun to experience the pleasures of living by consent, nor would you want it to be.

2
The Role of the Optimistic Parent

As I have already stressed, this book is not a recipe for neglect or permission for parents to 'let the kids get on what with it.' So where do parents fit in?

Powerful Parents

Parents have power over children and obligations to those children that the children do not have in return. This power is boosted by the natural desire of children to want their parents' approval. Parents decide to have children. The children have no say in this and do not enter into any form of contract to obey the parent merely by the act of being born or adopted. Parents, on the other hand, have a moral obligation to care for and help their children. This does not mean that building a home in which everyone wins is a matter of 'giving way' to every suggestion a child makes; rather, it is a matter of finding mutual solutions.

Trusted Parents

In a consent-based household, the parent is a source of morality, advice, information and helpful criticism. Living by consent does not mean that we should never make suggestions about information, activities, foods or anything else. It does not mean keeping our advice to ourselves, unless the child has heard it a hundred times and asks us to refrain from repeating it.

Sharing our ideas is an important, in fact vital, parental role. Of course some of our best ideas may be very good while others may, in fact, be awful, so we should not expect that sharing ideas will lead to compliance. We can share our assumptions about anything, even highly personal areas; hair color, body odor, room tidiness etc., provided that we are prepared to accept that in the final analysis some things are simply a matter of personal decision. A useful rule of thumb is that if we wouldn't expect an adult friend to comply, then we have no right to expect compliance from a child. Of course, Ben might welcome tips about personal hygiene before his first date, in which case there is a mutual solution. If we are willing to acknowledge our own limitations and if we are able to restrain ourselves from insisting, even when we are convinced that we are right, then our children are most likely to learn to look upon us as trusted advisors. They will realize that we don't know everything and that we sometimes speak unadulterated rubbish, but will ask for our opinion, knowing that they can do so without fear of compulsion. When children trust that criticism will not lead to compulsion, it is likely that parents will be given far more access to their children's lives than conventional parents. After all, lying or secretly engaging in dangerous behavior without ever seeking advice are not necessary to a child whose parents are not going to say 'no' on principal or threaten punishment.

One parent, Sue Cvach, suggested a very useful image for this kind of trusted parent; a sonar. Children can bounce ideas off a trusted parent, take soundings of their own depth and position from what is reflected back, and feel more equipped to make new decisions and try out new positions.

The Problem Solving Parent

Our ideas, information, moral views and criticisms are gifts, but it is up to the recipient to make best use of the gift. If that thought fills you with fear, think of it like this: When we insist that our ideas should be followed and when we threaten punishment or consequences (however 'liberally' conceived) we risk damaging our child's ability to think clearly and openly about the subject in hand. How can a child listen to reasonable arguments about teenage sex or eating chocolate or jumping from a ten-foot wall onto concrete if she really knows that ultimately the decision will not be hers, or she will have to resort to deception? On the other hand, if we offer good information then a child who is used to being respected will be more likely to see the logic of our argument on its own merits. If our argument is unconvincing, then perhaps more information is needed, or the child has a better assumption, or we're simply talking about a matter of taste and choice.

The Protective Parent

Of course we want to protect our children and be responsible parents, but I want us to consider that compulsion might not be a responsible course of action. Will compulsion ultimately keep children safe? What right has a parent to thwart a child's will in order to achieve the supposedly good end of protecting her? So how do we keep them safe?

Whether the protection is physical or verbal, it still requires that a mutual solution be found. Parents generally have a very much greater pool of life experiences to draw on. This can lead us to believe that we 'know best' or have a duty to compel 'for the child's own good'. This is not the case. Parents undoubtedly have more experience than children. And sometimes this will mean that we have good assumptions. It will also mean that we have accepted hundreds of bad and conventional ideas and may have had our own thinking damaged by the compulsion done to us as children. Experience is something that parents have to offer, but it is not always reasonable and right. Offering experience with acknowledgement of our limitations is a far cry from deciding that we know best.

We can offer our experience, without assuming it is infallible or universal and we can offer our best ideas, without presuming that we are correct, even if we deeply believe that on this occasion we are. We can give information and help our children to find other sources of information. Ultimately, having children who understand the decisions they are making as fully as possible and who know how to find out more information is eminently safer than having children who obey while their parents are there to impose their wills, but act in the dark as soon as they are on their own. From sharp tools to fires to staying out alone children who seek advice and who are used to coming to their own reasoned decisions are more safe.

Imagine two nine-year-old friends, Ashok and Luke. They are enjoying exploring a piece of woodland near their homes when one day they wander further and come across a derelict building. The building is boarded up, but not securely and they can wriggle inside. As they enter they pass a notice: 'do not enter, risk of falling masonry.' The building is full of wonderful hiding places and a great setting for imaginary adventures. Luke suggests they spend the day exploring the building and keep it their secret. Ashok already has a hundred ideas for games they could play in this new den, but says they should ask an adult to check that it's safe. He says that he knows that old buildings like this sometimes move or have rotted floorboards that give way under people. Luke replies that Ashok is chicken. He insists that they'll be fine and that adults are always telling children lies to stop children having fun. Luke also points out that if he asks his parents about playing here they'll just say no without even looking at the building and get mad with him anyway. Ashok objects that his parents don't tell him lies and that they like him to have fun. He says his Dad knows quite a bit about buildings and will be able to tell them how to play safely or find other ways for them to have a cool den if this building really is dangerous. Luke says angrily that adults don't help children, they just tell them what to do.

It is the child who has been brought up with rules who is much more in danger. Luke's information about the world is much less reliable that Ashok's. Luke's parents don't see fit to give him all the information; he just needs to know what he can and can't do. Luke also knows that not everything his parents tell him is true, he knows that they exaggerate or even fabricate to keep him in line, but he can't always tell the bogus from the vital information. Luke's parents have replaced information with rules, but Luke's desire to engage in illicit behavior is only increased by these rules. He sees his parents as the enemy and has a chance to outwit them. This attitude makes no sense to Ashok, who sees his parents as trusted advisors who will only give information that they really believe themselves. Ashok knows that whatever his parents think of this particular building, they will help him find a way of having a den and getting to play the games he and Luke want. Ashok knows that his parents help him to make his own mind up as though he is an autonomous person, not a silly idiot.

Luke, on the other hand, sees an opportunity to indulge in an activity that would be forbidden and that is so important to him that he can't think about the dangers or his friend's weird notion that adults help children. If Luke is wrong about the building, he could be in real danger. If Luke is right on this occasion, it is simply by chance, not as a result reasoned thinking, but this will only serve to entrench his idea that adults need not be consulted, which could mean danger now or later on for Luke, perhaps when he's fifteen and experimenting with drug use alone.

Having a child who will seek our advice before playing in a potentially dangerous place or conducting experiments with electricity or making their way out of an upper storey window is a great asset to safety. The conventional parent might insist that another thing that is extremely safe is to ensure that you have a child who just won't break the rules or is never allowed out of your sight. They might argue that Luke's parents have obviously not been strict enough and he should never have been in the woods in the first place. This is a hazardous argument. Some children are malleable; it takes only small amounts of compulsion to extinguish their drive to find their own solutions. Many children, however, are more resilient, and the force needed to impose external boundaries can make the home a virtual war zone.

Eighteen-month-old Tim, for example, has been told not to touch the fire. His parents begin by saying 'no' and trying to distract him each time he approaches. Tim continues to be interested, so the parents say 'no' more sternly and remove Tim to his bedroom for a few minutes each time he approaches the fire. Tim is undeterred, so his parents add a light slap on his hand on each occasion, but still to no avail. Now Tim's parents reluctantly, but for his own good, decide to spank him each time he tries to touch the fire. Tim is very distressed by this development, but does not give up. Where can these conventional parents go next?

Life in this household has become a long round of conflict. The fire will be just one of many battles being fought while the stakes escalate and everyone feels distress. If Tim's spirit of enquiry is not broken, eventually his energies will move into ensuring he does whatever he wants without being caught, and without advice and help.

Parents seeking their children's consent will examine their assumptions about fire. Is the fire a danger to Tim? Could he be protected by a guard and by showing him how different surfaces give off different kinds of heat? If the fire is a real danger, perhaps this is the problem that the parents should be addressing. In the meantime, they need to find ways to communicate the danger to Tim, ways to find a mutual solution that takes account of his safety and does not rely on lies or artificial rules that just beg to be broken.

Even if we manage to shadow our children relentlessly for many years, sooner or later they are going to be faced with making decisions and those who are likely to seek help with big decisions are much safer than those who relish every opportunity to defy and deceive their parents. We may succeed in making our children live by external rules, perhaps without resorting to heavy-handed punishments, perhaps by choosing our rules carefully and only imposing a few rules that will tend to hold in most cases. Even then, our children will not be as safe as children who are given honest information about risks, children who know that they can get all the help they need in negotiating risks, children who are accustomed to finding the best solution for any particular situation.

We can't foresee every situation. Life is risky, and there will always be tragedies whatever parenting method we use. Children will certainly take risks, but they will take them reasonably, advisedly, and with the best preparation to get the learning they want without exposure to unnecessary and unwanted danger if they are treated as serious people. Forcing children to accept external safety rules leaves them exposed and vulnerable to irrational decisions.

At five, Tim still loves to play with fire, but the rule is that Tim must not play with fire. Fire is dangerous. He could hurt himself or even burn down the whole house and kill the whole family. Two things could happen. The first is that Tim will find a way to secretly break the rule. In this case, he will either satisfy himself that his parents are telling lies and are not to be trusted, or he will have an accident of some nature, perhaps minor, perhaps more serious, but certainly avoidable if someone had helped him. The second is that Tim, finally crushed by the increasing severity of his punishments, will obey the rule and cease all exploration in this area. In the short term this may seem fine, but in fact Tim is left with irrational and untrue assumptions about fire that he will eventually pass on, and his own learning and curiosity in this area will have been cut off. Tim can't learn about fire, combustibility, the properties of materials and all the lines of inquiry that might arise from such experimentation.

In a consent-seeking household Tim's life would be completely different. His parents would give him good safety information about fire, outlining the possible dangers, but without exaggeration or pressure. They would explore the kinds of experiments Tim would like to do and discuss the best ways to go about them. They would assess together which experiments he could do alone, which would require help, what safety devices would be good to have on hand and where the best place would be to conduct the experiments. Tim could develop good assumptions about fire, pursue his own learning and stay safe.

Life and risks are bound together. Sometimes we choose risks quite reasonably in order to learn something or enjoy some particular experience, but many dangers are avoidable. The safest course is to parent our children so that they will trust our advice, critically assess our assumptions and make their own reasonable decisions.

The Engaged Parent

Let's be quite clear; abandoning children to their own devices without the constant input of information, moral beliefs and helpful criticism is a failure of parental duty. Any kind of parenting that carelessly leaves children to 'get on with it' is simply neglectful. Consent based parents are engaged parents. They ensure that their children have what they need to make well-informed decisions about their lives.

So, if it's not neglect, and our children are getting what they want out of life, then surely they can only be doing so at our expense? The assumption that parents and children are always in some way opposed and competing is false. Consent based parenting is not a call to parental self-surrender and martyrdom. What we are aiming at is consensual living and that means everyone, even you, the parent, should win. Living by consent does not mean becoming doormats with no lives. In fact, people generally find that when they begin eradicating compulsion from their relationships with their children, they are also less willing to live with compulsion in other areas of their lives. The adults are likely to begin expecting to be able to have their needs and wants met too, and it certainly can and should happen.

Of course we are talking about a long term process and we have to remember that we're only human. There are times when the mutual solution escapes us and we end up sacrificing our own desires to put children first. This is not ideal and it usually happens when we are tired, stressed or at our least resourceful. It is also more likely to happen when we first begin to try to live without compulsion or when we encounter an issue that we have not previously dealt with by consent. It is a solution that should and will be used less and less as we become practiced at problem solving.

Why is simply giving in and being the all-sacrificing parent such a bad solution? After all, parents are used to the notion that parenting is a sacrificial activity and self surrender is often held up as a virtue in society. Becoming the martyred parent is a bad solution because it prevents everyone involved from successfully problem-solving. When a mutual solution is found, everyone has continued working until they are genuinely pleased with the outcome. This creative activity produces new ideas and enlarges the family's thinking and confidence. If, at some stage of the process, the parent simply abandons their own desires, then they are robbing the family of ideas and resources, as well as short-changing themselves.

If this pattern continues, rather than being an occasional occurrence, then no one in the family will become practiced in finding mutual solutions. In place of win-win solutions, there will be the prevailing conventional notion that someone has to lose. The only difference is that now the parent is the loser instead of the child. We do not increase our children's ability to think and problem solve creatively by constantly stunting the problem-solving process. We do not show either our children or ourselves that win-win solutions are possible by agreeing to lose every time ourselves. Furthermore, we are likely to build up resentment towards our children if we continually give up our own wishes. This can often result in an explosion of compulsion when the martyr-victim-parent can stand it no longer, with an ensuing loss of trust in the whole process of finding mutual solutions. This is not a good outcome!

Unfortunately being the long suffering doormat is a built into many conventional notions of parenthood, with parents sometimes falling into the role of whining martyr and wondering why no one seems to care. Given that so many of us have models of this style of parenting from our own childhoods and since we may be accustomed to thinking that parenthood means sacrifice, it is hardly surprising that many parents who try to live by consent fall into the martyr syndrome. We desperately want to stop using force, but we are not used to the kind of innovative problem solving that achieves mutual solutions. In an attempt to avoid compulsion at all costs, we short circuit the entire process and just give in. Of course, it doesn't really help. Few of us can sustain martyrdom without either building up explosive resentment or resorting to manipulative remarks or subtle bids for control.

So, how do we know when we have become the martyr-parent and what can we do about it? We know that we are in a state of chronic martyrdom when we never or seldom prefer the outcome of any given problem-solving attempt. We know that we are stuck in this dead-end when we begin to think that it's inevitable that parents should feel this way. If we are telling ourselves that we must lose in order for our children to win, then we are definitely martyrs. It is likely that this will make the whole situation volatile, guilt ridden and liable to an ugly melt down at some stage.

Parents who continually self-surrender are not giving their children examples of problem solving or modeling how to get the best from life in the long term. This gives children little to look forward to as adults; they can hardly be blamed if they become grasping and uncaring when growing up looks so bleak. Whilst the children of self-surrendering parents become ever more insistent and demanding that their needs and wants are met this minute without question, the parents themselves are likely to become more and more depressed and resentful and ever less creative.

We can only begin to break this cycle when we convince ourselves that life doesn't have to be like this. If we believe that self-surrender is not noble, but actually draining and harmful, then we are more likely to resist it. If we are convinced that there are solutions out there, even when we fail to find them, then we are more likely to start again positively. If we are convinced that each family decision does not require that some lose whilst others win, we will not be satisfied with simply giving in. Instead, we will reserve self-surrender as a more and more infrequent default when all else fails us.

Consent works best when everyone in the family, adults and children alike, see themselves as free, respected people who can live the life they prefer within the family group. When this is happening, adults and children can all be open to changing their wishes without ever fearing that it will mean doing something they really don't want to do. This releases an enormous flood of problem-solving ability. To stop playing the martyr, we need to think seriously about what it is that we want. This doesn't mean that we have to become intransigent or unable to change our minds. We should start from what we want, not from what we don't want.

We should believe that we can get what we want, and communicate to our children that we can get what we want without in any way needing to trample on their wishes.

Children who are used to self-surrendering parents may be skeptical about this, but they will come to trust the process if they see that everyone can win, and that their parent's new found seriousness about their own needs is not going to be at the children's expense. In the longer term, children will be very happy to have a creative model of finding mutual solutions, which they know will serve them in continuing to get what they want as they move into adulthood. The future will look as flexible and full of possibility as the present.

Consider Sophie, aged three and her Mum, Lucy. Lucy grew up with a self-sacrificing, but highly manipulative mother. Her mother did everything for her all the way through childhood and her mother also complained continually about how she did everything and was unappreciated by her family. Lucy didn't learn to do any cooking at home; her mother said she would only make a mess and burn things, though no one ever let Lucy find out if this were true. She left home having never cooked an egg, hardly having ever boiled a kettle, not having a clue about washing her clothes and struggling to cope at college on her own.

Lucy is now a Mum herself and she does everything for Sophie, after all Sophie is so little and Lucy wants to be a good Mum. Unlike her own mother, Lucy doesn't resent her daughter. Two things have recently changed in Lucy's life: she has heard about consent based parenting and she has been offered some part time work doing research at home. Both appeal to Lucy, but Sophie is used to being served in every way. Sophie is a bright, happy little girl with lots of energy and interests and Lucy feels that Sophie should be able to play alone for at least short periods of the day, but Sophie calls on her continually,

"I need a drink, Mummy"

"Switch my video on, Mummy."

"Take me to the toilet, Mummy"

What's more, Lucy has noticed that Sophie's wants are very immediate; she wants what she wants and she wants it now. Despite all her vows never to end up like her own mother, Lucy can feel herself getting resentful, sometimes even snapping sharply when Sophie doesn't want to 'wait a minute' and then resenting all the extra time taken because Sophie gets upset.

Lucy talks to a friend who also tries to live by consent, and who makes some helpful suggestions. Lucy could buy some plastic jugs that Sophie can hold, fill them with her favorite drinks and water and keep them on a low refrigerator shelf that Sophie can reach. Lucy could teach Sophie how to operate the video and TV controls and how to go to the toilet alone. Lucy could spend some time in the morning with Sophie preparing snacks that Sophie likes and putting them in accessible places. Lucy could change the times when she works to evenings or weekends when Sophie's Dad can do something fun with Sophie while Lucy has quiet. She could offer to look after Sophie's best friend two afternoons a week in exchange for the same favor from the best friend's mum on another two afternoons. Lucy doesn't have to become Sophie's slave. It is quite likely that her daughter would enjoy being able to do at least some of the things for herself, but Lucy does have to think innovatively, not simply give up.

The Voluntary Parent

If you think that finding mutual solutions sounds like a lot of hard work, try asking yourself which form of parenting offers you an easy life. Parenthood carries responsibilities, but there is no need to see those responsibilities as terrible burdens. We can stop treating our relationships with our children as exacting demands and start enjoying them. We are sadly mistaken if we become parents thinking that there is an easy option. Relationships take work. Important relationships can take lots of work, but what would we rather work at – thwarting our children and constantly struggling to maintain control, knowing that it is going to involve a lot of negative conflict along the way – or helping our children to get what they want and getting our own wishes met, realizing that it is going to take a lot of resourcefulness? Trying to live by consent entails parenting in a counter cultural way which will demand that you are constantly creating new ideas; it is hard work and sometimes difficult to implement, but it is also an enormously satisfying and optimistic way to live.

Parenthood carries responsibilities, but that is not the same as sacrifice. If I pay for a holiday I don't think of the money I've used as being sacrificed. I certainly weigh up whether this is what I want to do with my money, but, having made the decision, I don't resent what I am giving up to get the longed-for holiday. Giving up the money in exchange for the holiday is voluntary, a simple way of getting something that I prefer and can enjoy more than the money in my purse. Children are not commodities, of course, and the analogy is limited; but, for parents, giving up certain aspects of a life without responsibility is not a sacrifice, but simply a shift to a new and preferred way of life.

We should enter into parenting with an intention to promote

our children's independence, delighted when we can help them get what they want from life, and thrilled that we can facilitate their growth, learning and happiness. This is not a burden or a sacrifice, but something parents prefer. When we start thinking and feeling like this, parenting ceases to be the chore that many conventional parenting theories would have us believe that it is. It is a sad reflection on our notions of parenting (and perhaps on our concept of relationships in general) that we confuse something which takes a lot of energy with something sacrificial, burdensome, and an occasion for resentment.

A swimmer who sets her heart on swimming a distance in a particular time has to devote a lot of energy, commitment and resourcefulness to achieving her goal. She does so willingly. She is happy to radically alter her diet and to devote her time to realizing her desire. Her goal is challenging and difficult, but it still remains voluntary; her most important preference and a joy. When we are able to see our relationships with our children like this, and not as onerous and tiresome, then we will not grudge the creativity and time that we put into finding mutual solutions. Rather, we will be exercising our wish to relate well to the child we chose to bring into the world or adopt. Finding mutually desired solutions is not galling, but delightful.

The Consenting Parent

Parents have wide-ranging roles in their children's lives:
* Parenthood comes with responsibility; you owe your children, they don't owe you.
* This gives you power that you can use for the good.
* The consent-based parent is a trusted advisor
* The final decision is theirs; you could be wrong
* Information and trust keep children safer than rules; the protective parent doesn't need to be the rule-bound parent.
* Leaving your children to fend for themselves is neglect; consent involves being an engaged parent.
* If you feel like a doormat, or can't remember what it's like to have a preference about something then you are a martyr and no one is going to win.
* 'Giving in' makes you resentful, stops your children from thinking of solutions and gives a poor picture of adulthood.
* If consent sounds like hard work, it is! But it's a great deal more pleasant than fighting your child for sixteen years.
* Helping our children can be a pleasure, not a chore.

3

The Power of Parenting Ideas

What stands in our way of living lives of consent? Most of us think that the obstacles are practical ones; we don't have enough time for all this innovative thinking, we don't have enough money to satisfy our children's wishes, we're not good at problem solving. We tell ourselves that our children are too young to be reasonable or that they have sugar allergies or soft teeth that mean we can't just let go of controls on their diet. The truth is that all of these practical problems are soluble.

Practical problems do not stop us from helping our child to get what he wants; ideas do. What gets in the way of living by consent is not schedules or the number of hours in the day or the need to go to work or the amount of money we have available, but the way we think; our resourcefulness, our ideas.

Imagine Paula. She is at the airport with her five-year-old daughter, Zoë, half an hour from boarding her flight from London, where her parents live, to Texas, where she lives. Suddenly, Zoë announces that she has left her favorite teddy bear at Grandma's house and she wants to go back to fetch it. Most of us in this situation think that the problem is one of time: we can't retrieve the bear and board the plane and it's obvious to any adult which of those things has to happen. If Paula is a conventional parent then she is probably willing to offer comfort to Zoë, as long as Zoë doesn't make too much noise in a public place, but Paula will also believe, like most parents, that Zoë has to learn that some things just can't be changed; some things just have to be done whether we like them or not; some things are simply not negotiable.

The real problem though is not the conjunction of practical factors; an airplane departure at 8.30 a.m.; a bear that is a forty minute round trip away and a distressed child do not add up to an impossible situation in which someone has to lose. The real problem is Paula's inability or unwillingness to think that there is a solution. The solution might involve a later flight. It is not actually an immutable law of nature that Paula and Zoë must get on this plane. As parents, we often present our decisions as though there is no choice, as though our doctor's appointment or need to do some grocery shopping is written into the universe, but the truth is that there are choices; as many as our resourcefulness allows us to envisage. On the other hand the solution might include Paula's initial wish that she and Zoë board their flight on time. Perhaps there is a story that they could invent together to make the bear's absence a good thing in Zoë's mind. Maybe they can agree that the bear is staying with Grandma so that she doesn't have to say good-bye to them all at once or maybe the story could be that the bear is being posted home as part of an adventure. Perhaps a new toy from the airport shop will make all the difference. Perhaps a call to someone at Grandma's house or to a courier service could get the bear to the airport in time. Perhaps Zoë simply needs more information about how much extra new plane tickets might cost, using up money she might like for other things or about how Daddy will be waiting at the airport in Texas and will be sad not to see them for another day. This information doesn't need to be delivered in a way that will manipulate Zoë with guilt and sentimentality, but as facts that she can take into consideration, knowing that the final decision has not already been made.

If Paula wants to live by consent with her child she will tell Zoë that she really strongly prefers that they make this plane. She will tell Zoë why she wants this, including things that she hopes to be able to do by being home at a particular time; people who are meeting them at the other end; extra expense and what that might mean to their family; effects on their tiredness and ability to enjoy an already long journey. She will make suggestions about alternatives; stories about the bear, a new toy, a trip to the ice-cream shop at the airport, the possibility of someone bringing the bear to the airport for them and how they will deal with it if the bear doesn't arrive on time. Zoë, knowing that her mother wants to find a mutual solution, will be able to listen and consider without feeling brow beaten, knowing that she doesn't have to sit on the airport floor and cry her heart out to get listened to.

Let's imagine that Paula is this consensual mother and she and Zoë find a solution. They decide to ring Grandma and ask her to post the bear, but they also ask Grandma to take some pictures of the bear at Grandma's house, the bear being packaged, the bear being handed in at the Post Office. Zoë and Paula take pictures together of their journey and decide to keep a scrapbook of things they do when they get home until the bear arrives so that they can make their own picture book of the days of the bear's adventure. In the meantime, an ice-cream, a large cuddly Dalmatian toy from the airport gift shop and the thought of Daddy waiting to meet them at the other end mean that Zoë happily decides to get on the plane now.

A couple of years later, Paula is at home with Zoë and her new baby, Jacob, when Jacob suddenly develops a high temperature and begins to convulse. The hospital is close to their home and Paula knows that she can drive there quicker than an ambulance would take to reach them and get back again. Zoë has just got a new play station game and Paula knows that Zoë really doesn't want to leave the house today, but neither is Zoë comfortable alone at home and Paula has noticed that both sets of friendly neighbors, who might otherwise sit with Zoë, have gone out today. Paula tells Zoë that this is an emergency, she doesn't have time to talk this through right now, but Jacob needs to get the hospital this minute. This is a very rare moment for Zoë; she knows that her mother doesn't lie to her, that Paula doesn't decide outcomes before discussions, so, despite not otherwise wanting to go to the hospital, Zoë has no qualms about accepting the genuineness of her mother's fears for Jacob and leaves her game without a backward glance.

Ideas, not practical problems are the real blocks to living by consent; solutions are out there, but we don't always find them because we don't always have ways of thinking about them. We all have inner voices that say 'you can't always win' or 'but teeth have to be brushed no matter what children want' or 'if Jimmie watches too much TV he'll become aggressive'. We all have areas in which our assumptions are constrained by the compulsion we experienced ourselves as children. These ideas can become so strongly held that they are ingrained in us and no amount of reason seems to shake them.

These deeply rooted ideas are well recognized and the scientist Richard Dawkins has given them a name that conveys the way these ideas reproduce themselves from brain to brain. Dawkins calls such ideas 'memes' and although these ideas are deeply embedded, we are not slaves to memes, we can work on them. So what is a meme?

Ideas that Reproduce

Dawkins talks about memes as being ideas that, like genes, self-replicate.

"Examples of memes are tunes, ideas, catch-phrases, clothes, fashions, ways of making pots or of building arches. Just as gene types propagate themselves in the gene pool by leaping from body to body via sperms or eggs, so memes propagate themselves in the meme pool by leaping from brain to brain via process, which, in the broad sense, can be called imitation. ...
Some memes, like genes, achieve brilliant short term success in spreading rapidly, but do not last in the meme pool. Popular songs and stiletto heels are examples. Others such as the Jewish religious laws, may continue to propagate themselves for thousands of years, usually because of the great potential permanence of written records." (From *The Selfish Gene*, by Richard Dawkins, Chapter 11)

So memes are simply the building blocks by which culture and ideas spread from one person to the next in learnt behavior or imitation. Dawkins uses the word memes to show how ideas reproduce in a similar way to genes. Like genes, memes are inherited; that is they are copied generation to generation. Sometimes the copying is not exact, but is subject to subtle or larger mutations and we select which memes will survive on the basis of whether they are highly memorable, useful or provoke an emotional response. In the arena of socio-biology there is a lot of argument about whether the theory of memes means that we are not free, but Dawkins himself and many others insist that we are free people.

The human arena of parenting is full of memes. Most of us have sworn never to be the kind of parents that our own parents were to us and yet most of us acknowledge that our most deeply rooted parenting ideas come from the way we were treated as children. Whether against our better judgment or not, we often discover that f our deepest held parenting assumptions not only bear more than a passing resemblance to those of our families, but also to the dominant theories of our particular culture.

Imagine Denise, for example. Denise's mother, Margaret, was firmly of the opinion that life was a competition that she and her family were fated to lose. Her own manipulative childhood and lack of education led Margaret to develop the idea that some people have to lose and she was such a person. As a protective mother, Margaret wanted to do all she could to stop Denise from getting hurt in the world, which for Margaret, with her constant sense of dread and low self-esteem, meant keeping a low profile.

If Denise showed an interest in a hobby or pursuit Margaret would seem initially interested and supportive, but she would soon begin suggesting that Denise might not really enjoy herself at ballet or horse riding or drama group; she might find it hard or fail and look silly, she might have an accident, she might not make friends. When the time came to take part in an activity, Margaret would soothingly tell Denise that she need not go if she didn't want to; she would sympathetically say that she understood that Denise didn't really like to be around too many people and shouldn't force herself to go. On later occasions Margaret would also refer to previous incidents to back up her theory that Denise had a history of not being able to cope with groups. 'Remember how you thought you'd go horse riding, but when it came to it you couldn't face all those strangers. I know you'd like to try things, but you always find groups so difficult. It's fine to stay home with me; maybe you shouldn't get involved with anything else.'

In time, Denise became more withdrawn. She learnt the meme that involvement in the world leads to failure and humiliation not because she failed herself, but because she was convinced by the ideas transmitted to her. Now Denise is a young mother and very protective of her four-year-old daughter, Helen. When Helen attempts to climb on the frame at the park, Denise hovers around, full of dread, constantly saying 'be careful', 'don't climb that high', 'mind you don't hurt yourself'. She notices that in interactions with other children Helen is always the child who has toys taken away from her or who hangs back on the edge of the group. Denise wants to help Helen have more enjoyment, but she is unaware of herself saying things like, 'It's only a toy, Helen, play with something else.' 'Never mind, darling, some people are like that, you just stay away from them.' 'You don't have to go to Sophie's birthday party. I know you don't really like parties.' Although Denise wants to help her daughter she is none the less acting out a meme that has passed down and, at four, Helen is learning not to expect too much from life and not to try to change things.

- Practical problems can be solved, but solutions are hard to find if our ideas stop us from thinking about them.
- Ideas that are passed on by behavior and imitation are called 'memes.'
- Memes (in the ideas world) are similar to genes (in the biological world); they evolve, they vary, they are selected if they are memorable or useful and they are passed on.
- Some memes survive for a short time, some for a long time. Those that do well tend to be highly memorable, useful or produce an emotional response.
- Memes exert a strong effect on parenting, even when we don't want to repeat our parent's mistakes

Changing our Parenting Ideas

Are memes so in control of our ideas that we can do little more than imitate the memes handed on to us by our parents or by our culture? Or can we come to recognize, criticize and change our memes? Like Dawkins, I believe that we can rebel; that we can use reason to consider the memes that operate in our parenting.

We have to remember that memes are not conscious. Ideas are not conspiring together to take control; it is simply that, as with genes, there is a process of selection in which certain ideas do well because of their features, like memorability or emotional impact. When we say that we are our memes, our ideas, we are not saying that we therefore have no control over our ideas. Our memes and ideas are essential to our resourcefulness and identity, but that does not make change impossible. As parents we may be acting under a range of memes that have largely been transmitted to us unwittingly. However this does not rule out our free-will, nor prevent us from being conscious, creative, and rational people who examine the ideas we live by.

- Memes, though not intentional, have the evolutionary urge to survive and propagate.
- Memes can have a powerful effect without our awareness.
- Memes are of differing kinds: some do not benefit us, some are neutral and others are beneficial.
- We can become conscious of our memes and exert our decision-making powers.
- We are not just victims of the ideas within us; we are rational and innovative.

Sifting through Parenting Ideas

Some of the most powerful and deeply ingrained ideas we have as parents are not just single ideas, but groups of ideas that work together. These have been called 'memeplexes' and examples are religions, ideologies, languages, alternative therapies and lifestyles.

Memeplexes will often contain many rational and useful ideas, but they will also contain false and harmful ideas that inhibit our thinking about children or lead to them being treated stereotypically and wrongly. In parenting, as in other areas of life we need to have a critical eye on the memeplexes as well as the individual memes.

One very common memeplex that occurs repeatedly in parenting is that of 'common sense.' A huge amount of compulsion is justified in the name of common sense. It is common sense that children have to learn to do as they are told; it is common sense that children have to go to school; it is common sense that children have to wrap up warm in cold weather; it is common sense that a child who doesn't learn to read by the age of ten is going to fail in life and so on.

Many of the memes that band together as 'common sense' and that aid one another's survival by this alliance, are questionable or false, but it is equally false to merely write off a whole memeplexe. The common sense idea that we shouldn't jump out of twenty storey buildings without a safety net is good advice that is not made less good by being lumped together with false common sense ideas. In other words, when we are dealing with memeplexes, it pays to be selective. We may want to reject the religion of our childhood or the political dogmatism of our parents, but it is worth sifting through the generations of memes that have survived to see where there are nuggets of truth.

Let's take Susan. Susan has adopted a 'natural living' memeplex that has greatly influenced her parenting. In this memeplex it is essential that babies are breastfed, carried everywhere (rather than pushed in prams or pushchairs), sleep in bed with their parents for as long as the baby desires, use only cloth diapers, wear natural cotton clothing, play with toys made from natural materials such as wood, not be exposed to TV and new technologies and eat a whole-food diet, particularly excluding refined sugars and processed foods. All seems well for Susan with her first baby, Pip, who responds positively to this lifestyle.

Later, Susan has another child, George, and, around the same time Susan hears about living by consent. Susan begins to think about the idea that she should be treating her children as unique individuals rather than according to a particular stereotype of what may or may not be 'natural'. This is a difficult concept for Susan, who has set up her life to do what she thought of as the very best for her children. She also finds that this second baby presents his own challenges to her former ideas. He is very unsettled in her bed, cries often and only appears to settle on those occasions when he is not held. George also suffers from constant nappy rashes, despite Susan's great care over cleaning and only using environmentally friendly washing powders. In desperation, she tries disposable diapers and the rash clears up (just the opposite of Pip who would get a rash on the rare occasions that Susan used disposables).

Susan begins to dramatically question the whole memeplex of 'natural living and parenting'. The more questions she asks, the more disenchanted she becomes with her former philosophy and increasingly skeptical. It would be tempting for Susan to simply throw out the whole memeplex; to believe that anything that she once thought natural is just a bogus control technique, but she would be wrong. Within the natural living memeplex are some important insights and when Susan has her third baby, Amanda, carefully sifting through individual ideas in the light of the unique person that Amanda is much more helpful. It so happens that Amanda, like Pip, has the kind of skin that prefers cloth diapers and it certainly seems that Amanda, like most babies, loves to breastfeed. Meanwhile, Amanda's older brothers are now benefiting from a house in which there is always plenty of fruit on hand, but where they can also access some sweet snacks too. Pip and George still enjoy their wooden toys, in fact Pip is beginning to show a particular interest in woodworking, but that doesn't stop the boys from also enjoying play station games.

Susan no longer believes that living by the memeplex of 'naturalness' is the best way to parent her children, but she can also see that the memeplex that she once thought held all the answers does in fact contain some very valuable insights.

- Memes group together to enhance their mutual survival
- Groups of memes, known as memeplexes, are transmitted in the same way as individual memes
- Memes survive for a reason, even if they are false and harmful.
- Memeplexes aid the survival of the memes that group together and within memeplexes that are both true and false ideas.
- When a particular memeplex is rejected there will still be good and useful ideas that are worth retaining.

Parenting Ideas: The Good, The Bad and The Ugly

How do we analyze memes and decide which are good or bad, true or false? We do so by using our reason and resourcefulness. However, we also have to proceed with some caution and humility. It would be easy to jump to the conclusion that if some memes are bad, even dangerous and harmful, then we should suppress these ideas in our children.

Linda, for example, is an active feminist who wants her daughters to appreciate their own self worth and to be able to feel confident and equal to any situation. However, to do this, she thinks that it is a good idea to limit their access to books and TV shows that stereotype girls and women or which portray violence against women. Linda knows that bad ideas can do harm and so she wants to protect her daughters from such bad ideas, reasoning that free speech and an uncensored environment is not always worth the price of the harm done when bad ideas spread unchecked.

Linda is correct to think that some ideas do harm. It is also undeniable that free speech and a lack of censorship give bad ideas the chance to spread, but she is still wrong to censor her children's environment and to decide for them how to assess ideas. Some ideas are wrong, but limiting other people's freedom not only suppresses 'wrong' ideas, it also suppresses critical thinking and stops good new ideas from emerging. Ultimately, Linda's daughters will need to be able to hear, withstand and argue against the bad ideas that demean them as women if they are to have any power to effect new ideas.

Memes are variable; good, bad and ugly. We carry many memes unwittingly, but that does not stop us from rebelling, from choosing which memes will inform our parenting and which will damage the process. Neither does it give us the right to stop our children from encountering bad ideas; they, like us, need to have access to the full range of ideas in order to be able to discriminate and make reasonable and innovative judgments.

The trick to deciding for ourselves which memes are good or harmful in the arena of parenting is, I want to suggest, by using our reason and ingenuity to constantly test out which ideas stand up to questions. A useful question to ask of our parenting ideas is, 'Who benefits?' By treating our children as unique and by living in consent-seeking ways with our children so that everyone benefits, everyone wins, we can make better and better distinctions about which memes are helpful or harmful.

Part 2:
A World of Improvement

Ideas can limit us, but we are not their puppets; we can fight back. In this part of the book I want to examine a range of conventional parenting ideas such as 'children need to be told what to do;' 'you can't always have what you want;' 'frustration is character building' to begin questioning everything we've been told about parenting. Along the way I'll use practical examples to illustrate how things can be different; how living by consent can continually improve family life.

Each of the next eight chapters looks at a different group of ideas or memes that can be obstacles to achieving consent and how we can overcome them. In chapter four I will look at the nagging notion that consent simply isn't for children. All too often we are left thinking that children are too flawed or self destructive; too heavenly and in need of protection; too prone to failing or have character traits which make compulsion in their best interests, but we don't have to buy into these ideas.

In chapter five I will examine doubts about getting what we want, the inner voices that tell us that we have to lose and need to suffer as part of character formation. In chapter six I will deal with some traditional theories about the role of parents as authority givers, boundary setters and responsible controllers before going on, in chapter seven, to facing those fears that tell us that children will become monsters unless they are controlled. In chapter eight I will discuss some of the practicalities of living together by consent; saying more about the parental role, as well as exploring parental expectations and children's behavior. In chapter nine I will consider how living by consent might affect other areas of life, particularly learning and the goals we have for our children. I will move on, In chapter ten, to consider how we can live by consent in the real world and what questions this might raise in situations of emergency or in relation to how children's futures might be affected. Finally, in chapter eleven, I will look at the selfish reasons for parents to live by consent before summing up in chapter twelve.

Throughout these chapters I want to invite you to question everything you have ever thought about being a parent, suspend disbelief and imagine that everything might not be as you have been told. There are plenty of people who will go on telling you that 'children sometimes have to be forced to do or be certain things,' but, as the songs say, not only is "It ain't necessarily so.", but with a life of consent "things can only get better."

4
Only Human

At various times there have been particular groups of people whose humanity and rights were undermined by ideas that stereotyped and denigrated them as a group. Black people are one such group. Some of the false ideas were so tenacious that we still see the surviving memes at work in racisms today. The false ideas tended to be of different kinds; there were the kind that blatantly doubted that black people were as intelligent or even as human as white people; there were the kind that infantilized black people, casting them as too child-like or primitive to warrant self determination and claiming that it was in their best interests that white people should make important decisions for them; there were even the kind that romanticized black people, the noble savages who should only live primitive lives, so that white people could have some imaginary link back to a world unsullied by the progress that they themselves were benefiting from.

In other times and cultures it has been women who have suffered from similar false ideas. The problem with such ideas was that they kept whole groups locked into stereotypes and so stifled progress, innovation and individuality. They were a waste of human life, which is in fact impossible to categorize, label and control. More and more, however, everyone's humanity and individuality is recognized and respected. We can recognize the talents of a black musician without having to believe that every black person has some mystically innate sense of rhythm; we can support a woman's decision to be a stay at home mother without having to believe that education is wasted on women, who are all little more than baby-machines. We are increasingly able to take a more complex view of real people and their multiple identities, unless, of course, they are children.

Children have certainly benefited from progress. We do hear people talking about children as unique individuals, but despite this, children are still much more likely to be categorized and stereotyped as a group than any adult population, not merely by extremists (after all, sadly, black people are still subject to racisms and women to sexisms in varying measures) but in general. In the Western world children's lives have improved enormously. They have more access to information, more buying power, more opportunities to articulate their preferences than at any other time in history. Indeed, Western children are often deemed as having so much that some people think that children would be more content if they had less in their lives. So am I really suggesting that children don't have enough? Am I arguing that children are the last oppressed minority?

I don't want to say anything so simplistic. Children in affluent countries have gained a great deal from being alive today. Children do have more, and long may it continue and spread to those with unequal access to the world's resources. Children are more likely to be seen as individuals than ever before, and that too is good. However, it is still the case that in parenting, certain ideas persists which fundamentally undermines our wholesale acceptance of children as full human beings. Children still suffer from ideas that once uniformly affected black people or women at other times. In this chapter I want to examine four groups of ideas that are still alive and well and stereotyping our children to their detriment.

The notion that children are born bad, can't be trusted and must be civilized is powerful and widespread. It originates in a sub-section of religious ideas, but it is an idea that has spread into popular thinking. It is an idea that needs to be challenged.

Not everyone has such a negative view of children, but many people do have the idea that children, if not bad, are not quite the finished article. It seems to be a matter of common sense that children's lack of experience renders them somehow 'lesser' and unable to know what's good for them. Common sense is very often not sense at all, just the residue of the bad ideas we had foisted on us when we were children, to paraphrase Einstein.

Others take a much higher view of children. Sadly, this isn't always helpful, as it can tend to make children into romanticized stereotypes rather than unique individuals. 'Magical' children don't eat sugar, watch TV or play with plastic guns. Like women before them, children afflicted by this crippling meme find that the pedestal is a place with little room to maneuver.

Of course, many people don't think of children as born bad and nor do they romanticize and chain children to the pedestal, they may not even distrust human nature in general, but they do distrust some people. This more specialized distrust easily becomes a rationale for control, particularly when it comes to certain categories of children; boys or hyperactive kids for instance. In such cases it is all too common to hear that reasonable negotiation and problem solving will be of no use here. Whilst pressure groups and increasingly enlightened thinking extends more and more of the dignities of humanity to vulnerable groups like Alzheimer's patients, geriatric patients, disabled people etc. (and rightly so) there are certain groups of children whose chances of being treated seriously as individuals are considerably worsening. The rash of forcibly medicated children ostensibly suffering from ADHD is a prime example, but similar memes are at work whenever certain children are lumped together as a stereotypical group to be treated according to some formula rather than as unique individuals.

Children Are Not Born Bad.

The idea that we are all born 'bad' started life as a religious doctrine, but, over the years, it has become established in popular thinking; most of us have heard people say that from their first moments babies are out to manipulate and out-wit us as adults. Being self willed, strong willed, having powerful basic needs or exhibiting distress whenever preferences aren't being met are commonly interpreted as signs that even the youngest baby is potentially a monster seeking to control us unless we show him who is boss. Selfishness is rarely seen as something good and creative (a subject to which we will return in chapter 5), but instead is viewed as a kind of declaration of war and a signal that the parent is about to be asked to lose. For some, selfishness can even be taken as a signal that the child is on the slippery slope to self-destruction or hell.

None of this is true. If we assume that a child's will is a bad or dangerous thing then we are saying that the human condition is essentially one of moral deformity with an inbuilt bias towards always doing the wrong thing. We are saying that it inevitably takes some kind of force (whether physical or psychological) to keep children from doing harm to themselves and others. We are buying into the idea that children, in fact all of us, are fundamentally bad. What makes us believe that children are bad?

Experience? Experience is largely a matter of perspective. Having children who are strong willed and who resist our commands may be a sign that children are fundamentally independent human beings with their own minds and a right to their own will. Having children who make terrible mistakes may be a sign of their limitations or their lack of access to good quality information. It may be a signal that such children have their thinking about morality badly damaged, but it does not make all children inherently bad.

Imagine Frances. She is a normal six year old in an ordinary family. Frances' mother, Gina, is very worried about her because Frances is becoming more and more aggressive towards her younger brother Simeon, aged 2. Only yesterday, Frances hit Simeon across the face when he walked across a picture she was painting and today Gina has had to send Frances to her room when she started screaming at Simeon for messing with the TV remote whilst Frances was watching a favorite video. Gina has also noticed that sometimes Frances is not merely 'over-reacting', as she terms it, but is instigating conflict; teasing Simeon when he can't pronounce words properly, even pinching him when she thinks no-one is looking.

Most of Gina's friends tell her that this is normal sibling rivalry and that Frances has to learn to share and be tolerant of younger children. However, Gina's friend, Mary, is trying to live by consent with her children and she suggests that the problem is that Frances has learnt that someone always loses. If Simeon is allowed to play freely in the dining room, then she can't paint or build a complex Lego model. If Simeon can explore unhindered in the living room, then the best she can hope for is a series of frustrating interruptions when she's watching a video. Frances doesn't expect her mother to defend her toys or space because she is supposed to be the 'big girl'. Instead, Frances has to defend herself and she sees Simeon as the enemy. Simeon not only ruins her fun constantly, but he has also taken first place in their mother's attentions and cost her Gina's approval. Frances is in an almost constant state of distress, Mary suggests, and as long as the idea that someone always has to lose persists in the household then Frances is going to continue doing harmful things in a vain attempt not to always be the loser. Gina is taken aback by this and has lots of objections:

Is Mary suggesting that Frances be allowed to get away with hurting Simeon?

No. Of course Gina should explain her moral ideas about not hurting people to her daughter. However, doing so by telling her that she is bad or a naughty girl in the heat of the moment is hardly likely to make Frances feel more reasonable and able to improve her reactions. The time to share moral information is when things are calm, perhaps as part of a wider discussion when an opportunity presents itself; perhaps as a conversation arising from one of Frances' favorite videos, Snow White, when the jealous stepmother plots to have Snow White killed.

Gina can also apologize to Frances and let her know that she understands that things need never have become this bad if she herself had helped the children to find solutions.

Surely, if Gina stops compelling Frances to stop hitting Simeon then the violence will just escalate?

Only if Gina persists with the idea that someone has to lose. What Gina can do instead is explain to Frances that she wants things to change; that she realizes that she hasn't been helping Frances to solve her problems with Simeon and so Frances has been unhappy. Gina can explain that from now on she does want to help and she wants everyone to be happy with the solution. There is no magical way to achieve this goal, but believing that problems are capable of resolving to everyone's liking is an excellent start.

Surely, Frances will take this new regime as a signal that she has won and she will feel able to get away with anything?

Frances should feel that she has won, but that is not the same as feeling that now it is Simeon's turn to lose or that immoral behavior works. Gina is not offering to let Frances beat up Simeon whenever he annoys her. She should share her moral ideas. She should protect Simeon from harm. It is simply that the energy of the family is now going into finding solutions that everyone wants, instead of going into blame and punishment.

Once Frances has begun to see how mutual solutions can be found, she will have more trust and be more open to contributing to finding mutual solutions; she will be more ready to help Simeon get what he wants too, since after all, it is not going to detract anymore from her fun and learning. Frances is not being turned into a 'spoiled brat', but assisted to become her reasonable and creative best.

Having experience of children who are resistant to our compulsion or who make bad decisions is not the same as having children who are, in essence, bad. The idea that children are simply born 'bad' is harmful and demonizes children. It is a concept that sets up a power struggle in which we as parents are playing for extremely high stakes. We find ourselves thinking that if we do not control our offspring, if we do not find effective ways to discipline them, then they will never become civilized, they will never be tamed, house-broken and trained in the ways of decent living, but will turn out to be immoral louts.

This is a frightening prospect for parents and it is little wonder that they run to titles like *Dare to Discipline* or *Toddler Taming* in their millions. Parents care about their children; they genuinely want to do the best they can and if they believe that human nature has a propensity towards immorality then they will easily be convinced that they are all that stands between their children and moral ruin. Life is full of mistakes. We are all limited. Laboring under assumptions that scare parents and which lead to children being compelled, however, isn't a solution. Children are not bad; they are merely human; ordinarily human with all the reasonableness, resourcefulness and thirst for learning that any human has.

How we parent our children depends on how we view them. If humans are not born bad then what is there to fear? If humans are born reasonable and creative as well as limited, then why should we need to rely on obedience as a parenting tool? In fact, obedience is a very dangerous commodity; it aids tyrants and fosters atrocities. If we think carefully about something that someone else wants us to do and decide that it is the right thing to do and that it fits in with our values and assumptions, then it is not obedience, but a preference. If we do it against our will and better judgment, then we are in a state of compulsion and are acting irrationally. Bringing up irrational children who will obey the person who shouts loudest isn't what most parents are aiming for.
In short:

- Children are limited, not bad.
- Selfishness is not the same as being self-destructive or immoral. (more about this later)
- Obedience and irrationality go hand in hand.
- We can reason with our children, share our best ideas and help them to find all the information they need to make good decisions.

Children Lack Experience, Not Humanity

The idea that children will tend towards the bad if they are not controlled is so deeply ingrained in our culture and thinking that it has taken on the appearance of something obvious and self-evident even when we rationally don't believe it. The result is that even when we think we are rid of this meme we often labor under similar ideas; children lack experience so they can't make decisions, children lack the ideas to behave morally without the pressures of civilization, and so on.

What is more often the case is that we set up self-fulfilling vicious cycles. We observe that some children become immoral when the controls are lifted from their lives, without considering whether the controls were what damaged their thinking and morality in the first place. We cannot systematically compel children to do as they are told, take away their abilities to be reasonable, creative, self-determining people and then claim that we were right to distrust them when we see examples of bad decisions. All we have shown is that we are able to create self-fulfilling vicious circles.

Moreover, observation is often a poor way to draw conclusions about human nature. So often, we see what we want to see and we end up thinking that a whole range of family conflicts from sibling rivalry to teenage rebellion are inevitable stages to be endured, justifying compulsion along the way. This leaves many families living from one problem phase to the next. The whole of childhood becomes a series of difficult stages that parents have to control as best they can in order to end up with young adults who are civilized enough to repeat the cycle again with their children.

I want to suggest that we can live by another theory. The theory is that:

- although humans are limited this does not have to lead to a life of conflict, because:
- self-interest is a good thing that can benefit individuals, families and society alike
- and everyone can win without parents needing to fear that their children will become anti-social monsters.

It might be 'only human' for a child to want what she wants, but does that make it a bad thing? Does that mean that someone else has to lose? Living by consent is about creating the conditions in which everyone can win.

Let's take Ned. Ned has been a 'difficult' child for a long time. As a toddler he was extremely strong willed and got into everything. Ned broke ornaments, drew on the walls, tormented the cat and generally caused a whirlwind of havoc wherever he went, including the local playgroup, where he was soon unwelcome because he would kick, push and take toys from other children. Ned's mother tried spanking him, but it merely seemed to provoke enormous rages and she was aware that escalating the violence was not a solution.

At school things got considerably worse. Ned could not keep still and was often rude and aggressive. After agonizing months of intrusive family therapy in which Ned's parents often felt under terrible scrutiny and judgment, Ned was finally diagnosed with ADHD and medicated with Ritalin. Ned's parents felt relieved to have the diagnosis, they felt it absolved them from blame; there was something wrong with Ned, not them. However, even medication didn't solve the problem completely. Ned still had violent outbursts and temper tantrums that were increasingly scary as he grew bigger and stronger. He still broke things in rages and he seemed to be learning very little at school.

By the age of nine, Ned's teachers were talking about a special unit and Ned's mother was becoming increasingly depressed. A day never passed without incidents, time-outs and withdrawal of privileges, such as watching TV programs, playing video games or going out to play with friends, but this never seemed to have the desired effect. The crunch came for Ned's mother when she discovered that she was unexpectedly pregnant again. Ned became even more aggressive and got into trouble for bullying other children at school, which ended in him being suspended. He then began frightening his mother with grim fantasies about how he intended to harm the new baby when it was born.

In a desperate attempt to find some advice Ned's mother, Gill, came across the idea of parenting by consent. The advice seemed extra-ordinary. Could any sane person suggest that, given total latitude, Ned simply wouldn't behave in these horrible ways? Changing from a conventional parenting style, especially when the damage is so overt, to an environment of reasonable and creative problem solving in which everyone wins is certainly no easy task. Given Ned's history of perpetrating so much damage on property and people, it is hardly surprising that his mother would be understandably taken aback at the suggestion that she should stop trying to force her son to do things and help him to get what he wants. Yet the argument remains that if Ned had been brought up in a consent seeking environment he would not be as he is. Why would a child whose independence is nurtured need to throw tantrums or wreak havoc and destruction? Children in consensual households know that they can have their preferences met without having to resort to immoral behavior or expecting anyone else to lose. Yet even if this is the case, it is patently obvious that Ned has not been brought up in this way and has developed lots of ways of hurting other people.

The objections to change are legion:

If such a child is given freedom, then surely he will misuse it?

It is true that this is a very bad situation. It is reminiscent of the traveler who asks directions only to be told, 'if you want to get to there I wouldn't start from here.' The first thing that Ned's parents can do is to apologize. They can tell him that they want to stop hurting him and start helping him. They can tell him that they do not believe he is a faulty product who can never be as good as anyone else, but now understand that he has been harmed by all the compulsion used against him and from now on they want to find ways for everyone to win.

The likelihood is that Ned is not going to believe this

straight away and he may even put the new regime to the test, making some very bad decisions and straining his parents resolve to the limit.

So what if Ned does something so dangerous that his parents simply have to use compulsion?

Ned's parents are limited and they too are learning. Compulsion happens in all families; no one is perfect, but Ned's parents shouldn't use this to justify compulsion. If compulsion happens because of some very real and dire emergency then Ned will probably be able to understand the action, but such emergencies are much rarer than we often imagine, even in families like Ned's. If compulsion happens because his parents lose the struggle to change and temporarily lack the resourcefulness and reasonableness to problem solve in a stressful situation, then it is because they are ordinary human beings trying to do the best with the knowledge they have available. They can apologize to Ned, discuss what they have learnt, and talk about how they could handle a similar situation on another occasion.

This situation is hard. Making the shift will help enormously, but it won't happen overnight. The whole family is going to be engaged in finding new ideas and that is difficult. There will be failure and times of doubt and frustration, but just as we don't expect to put out a fire by lighting more fire nor can we expect to start living by problem solving, consent and mutual solutions by using compulsion. Adding compulsion to a situation already loaded with compulsion damage will not help. Over time the family will see changes; every success at finding mutual solutions will generate more resources for solving the next problem. Gradually the family's energy will become solution oriented instead of failure oriented.

Surely, if Ned is so irrational and damaged he is going to demand the freedom to do bad things?

Children are as limited as adults. Children who have experienced a lot of compulsion may very well be irrational or make bad choices. Acting against Ned's wishes, however, isn't going to help him to become more reasonable. If there is a good reason for Ned not to do something then it should be possible to communicate this through reason. If this can't be done then perhaps the reason for not doing something doesn't really bear scrutiny.

Let's assume however that Ned's parents have presented him with a good reason not to do something. For example, Ned has had a series of very late nights. By the fifth of these nights Ned can barely keep his eyes open and he is complaining of feeling sick and showing signs of being emotionally fragile. Ned's parents have explained that they think his sickness and feeling low are signs of his need for sleep and that he is hurting himself, but he wants to hear the end of a story that his Dad has been reading to him and this could take another hour. His Dad doesn't mind reading the book, but he is very concerned that Ned might be making himself ill and even more concerned that Ned might start to get moody and aggressive if he gets any more tired.

The fact remains that a child behaving irrationally is not a sufficient justification for risking the harm that compulsion might cause. It is fine to give information and offer alternatives. It is very good to treat Ned carefully and gently whilst he's feeling so tired, but the decision to sleep or not has to be his. It may be Ned is making the wrong decision, but on the other hand it could be that despite Ned's tiredness, nausea and sensitivity he is really making a very good decision. Perhaps he is learning a great deal from the story he is hearing as well as forming valuable new assumptions about his ability to trust that his parents' advice is not going to be followed by compulsion if he doesn't take it. Deciding that Ned is behaving irrationally assumes that we can see into the minds of others. We can't. We might be right or we might be wrong, but either way, adding in more compulsion is not going to produce a change to living by consent.

- We are all limited; adults and children alike, but the fact that children make bad decisions sometimes is not sufficient reason to think that they are bad or to deny their right to make decisions.
- Compulsion damaged children will make mistakes, but creating the conditions for consent and mutual solutions is infinitely more helpful than adding in more compulsion.
- Children are limited, in need of information, and less experienced than adults, but they are equally creative, reasonable and human.

Children Are Not From Heaven

The memes that tell us that children are bad or that the human condition is one that tends to destructiveness are highly questionable, but, oddly, they co-exist alongside another set of memes that would have us put our children on pedestals. Such ideas have been used on others, as I've already mentioned. The idea of the 'noble savage' defined black people in what sounded like glowing terms, but turned out to entail vast limitations on their personal autonomy, dignity and progress, supposedly, and quite wrongly, for their own good. Benevolent dictatorship is still dictatorship and people know when they are in cages, no matter how fine the gilding.

One of the most pervasive of romanticized false memes effecting children today is the idea that children are closer to nature and so they should be kept that way, protected from refined sugar or TV viewing or plastic toys or anything that might detract from their unsullied natural state.

In *Magical Child* Joseph Chilton Pearce, for example, sets out a theory of children's minds and nature's plan for intelligence which relies on us limiting children's experiences with the intention of ending up with idealized geniuses. Although the intentions are meant to be for the greatest good of the children, what results is that children are treated not as unique individuals, but as a homogenous group who can be raised according to a formula. This leads to blanket decisions about what children can do that takes no account of individuality; TV is outlawed for young children and reasoning with young children is scorned as not, 'allowing children to be children'.

Such theories evoke a backwards looking golden era, that few of us can hope to recreate even if we wanted to (quite aside from arguemnts about whether such a golden age ever existed.) Children are not our umbilical cord to a mythical, romantic past in which humanity once lived at one with nature. Undoubtedly books like Jean Liedloff's, *The Continuum Concept* have done a great deal of good by increasing support for breastfeeding or co-sleeping arrangements with babies and young children. Many of the features of parenting described by Liedloff as 'natural' are what many babies and families prefer, but good ideas can become harmful once they are made prescriptive or imply that anyone who deviates is not 'normal' and 'natural'. Sadly, authors like Liedloff and Chilton-Pearce take nature much more seriously than they do children.

Liedloff extols the harmony of the Yequana, but never questions the morality of obedience and conformity nor the rigid elder-younger and male-female hierarchies that this maintains. In such a conformist culture, there is a remarkable lack of innovation. The tribe continues to solve the same problems in the same ways. Such a static lack of problem solving is deeply conservative and stifling to the kind of self-fulfillment that we have the opportunity to nurture in our children. We don't need to aspire to live like Stone Age people in order to be good open to taking the best ideas from other cultures where they fit with our individual children's preferences. Rather, what we need is to recognize that every human person, even the youngest, is a human being worthy of being treated as a unique individual.

Let's consider Dylan. By the time Dylan is born his mother. Brooke has already decided how things are going to be. Dylan will be carried everywhere, breastfed for at least two years, progress only to organic, sugar free foods, play with the most beautifully crafted wooden toys, wear cotton and never watch TV, play computer games, join in any nasty gun play games nor follow the latest consumer crazes for children.

Dylan's birth is not the idyllic water birth that Brooke had planned, but turns out to be a caesarian section. Brooke is understandably disappointed, but she is also besotted with her perfect baby boy and soon finds breast feeding everything she had imagined. Dylan also enjoys being carried in his anatomically designed sling and the cloth diapers, cotton clothing and wooden rattles seem to work well for him. At night, however, things are not so smooth. Dylan is fretful and hot all through most of each night, but doesn't want to feed more than once. Brooke's partner, Richard, gently suggests putting Dylan in a crib by the bed, but Brooke resists until she is so exhausted one night that she finally lets Richard take over. Put down alone, Dylan falls asleep and wakes only once, six hours later. After feeding him Brooke snuggles him against her, but Dylan frets until Brooke puts him back into his own space, where he falls instantly asleep.

Aside from seeming to prefer to sleep alone, Dylan shows no signs of discomfort with any other aspect of his life in the first few months. He is an extremely contented baby and, at six months, he begins eating pureed organic banana, organic yoghurts and pureed vegetables. By the age of two Dylan is an easy going, bright toddler. Although Brooke is a little disappointed that Dylan refused to breastfeed beyond the age of ten months, she remains convinced that her natural parenting techniques are going to see her and Dylan through the coming years. She is also delighted to have a second baby, Ashley, a little girl who loves sleeping in her mother's bed.

Brooke tries out some local mother and toddler groups, but she is soon disappointed. The toys are generally garish plastic; the snacks are not rice cakes and fruit, but biscuits, and the drinks are not watered down organic fruit juices, but squash laced with additives. Some of the other mothers are very friendly and Brooke is glad of the company, but she is very anxious about the influences of the modern world on her son's natural development. When one of the mother's invites her round for coffee she arrives to find a video ready for the children to watch, a house full of plastic toys and a computer sitting in the corner of the living room. Back at home, Dylan, says he wants a TV and toy guns and swords like Carl's.

Brooke has to choose. At two, it's going to be increasingly difficult to keep Dylan cocooned away from the world of TV, sugar, toy guns and computer games. She is either going to have to re-examine her ideas or accept that in order to keep Dylan 'natural' she will have to carefully hand pick his friends and she will need to do a lot of work to convince Dylan that the fun Carl is having watching videos, playing pretend fight games and eating chocolate ice cream is actually really bad for him. She is also going to have to face the possibility that as Dylan gets older he will manage to access some of these fun activities by subterfuge, relying less and less on Brooke as his trusted adult adviser. She has to decide whether to raise Dylan by the book, trusting in the authority of nature as it is transmitted to her by romantic modern writers like Pearce or whether she is going to raise Dylan as Dylan; unique and free-thinking.

Being allowed to develop naturally can sound exactly like being free to develop freely, but the two are not the same. Natural development is actually strictly controlled according to a preordained agenda of what it means to be 'natural'. Projecting any 'mystical', 'unspoilt' qualities onto children is ultimately demeaning. It traps children in an adult, romanticized fantasy of what it means to be a child.

- Our children are not bad, they are not little devils; fallen and corrupt, but neither are they innocents with an intuitive sense of angelic goodness and an innate closeness to nature.
- It may be romantic to think that men are from Mars, women are from Venus and children are from Heaven, but the truth is: people are from Earth. The best we can do is get used to it and find ways to live together by consent.
- Finding consent is not only hampered by demonizing our children, but also by idealizing them.
- We need to see children as like ourselves: unique, but limited human beings.

Boys Will Be People

Limited, yes; most of us have no problem with that. Self-directing? Perhaps for some children, but surely there are those who don't respond to reason, who simply need a lot of control? I want to argue that consent is for all: even green-eyed, ginger haired children, born on Wednesdays and suffering from left-handed syndrome, can live by consent. Let's unpack that idea.

Many parents that I speak to about living consensually with children are attracted to the idea of finding win-win solutions to family problems. However, many are also reticent to let go of certain ideas about particular groups of children. There is often a belief that whilst girls might respond well to the process of finding mutual solutions, boys are another species, who are much more difficult to raise and much harder to reason with. Others assert that there are children who by nature are more difficult and require control, usually children diagnosed as having such conditions as ADHD or Asperger's Syndrome. Consent really is for all, which is not to say that we should ignore particular characters, but merely to assert that we find consent by addressing people as individuals, not as examples of a group to which they may or may not belong. We need to stop thinking of unique individuals as representatives of a stereotypical group who are merely 'acting out' pre-determined challenges which beg for adult discipline.

In *Raising Boys* Steve Biddulph says that boys are different; they are driven by testosterone, have different brains and go through three distinct developmental stages. They begin in infancy with their mothers, move on, between 6 –13, to a state when they need their fathers to actively model how to be men and finally from 13 need adult mentors outside their families if they are ever to grow into responsible and caring adults who will not depend on alcohol or drugs or become despairing non-achievers. Well, yes, access to trusted adults is certainly pivotal to having good information from which to make good decisions and fathers as much as mothers clearly have vital roles, although trusted adult figures are not always going to be the biological parents. Gender may be one very important factor in how we relate to another person, but it is not the whole picture and should not be used to pigeonhole people or limit their freedom and individuality.

In contrast, William Pollack, author of *Real Boys, Rescuing Our Sons From The Myths of Boyhood* identifies three myths. Firstly he challenges the notion that nature and specifically testosterone controls much of boys' behavior making them prisoners of their own biology. He concedes that testosterone does play a part in the tendency for boys to love action and rough play, but also notes that its effects vary enormously. One boy might be aggressive whilst another is highly single minded, giving him an intellectual focus. Pollack argues that it is not testosterone, but parental love and nurturing that is the major factor in how boys grow. Secondly, he challenges the myth that "Boys SHOULD be Boys" In other words,

> "there is no one correct pathway to healthy masculinity."

Thirdly he takes issue with the myth that boys are "inherently dangerous or toxic". Boys are not naturally more unaware or unsocialized, or emotionally insensitive.

Biology is undoubtedly one of the assumptions that a person has about himself or herself. Biology, no doubt, has an impact on who we are, but trying to define the precise scope of that impact amongst the many cultural and environmental factors that make up a person is a losing game. It may feel very convenient to be able to relate to our child as an example of the species 'boy', and it may even appear to 'work' to some extent, but ultimately an individual is just that.

Take Adrian, for example. As a young child of about four Adrian, who has three younger sisters, expressed an interest in music and dance. He began to play the recorder and later the flute and attended ballet classes that he kept up long after he became the only boy in the class. As a teenager of 14, Adrian no longer dances; he's grown into a tall, broad young person and feels that he has taken this interest as far as he wants, but he still loves watching ballet. He still plays the flute and has also developed a keen interest in art; especially very fine miniature drawings. Another passion of Adrian's is history and he loves attending battle re-enactments and has a keen interest in mediaeval weaponry and tactics. In his spare time Adrian spends hours at his computer playing warfare and fantasy role-playing games.

Does Adrian like war games so much because his body is fueled by testosterone? Well, he is certainly going through the physical changes of adolescence, but one of his sisters, ten year old Ruth, seems to like the same games just as much and two of his three sisters love to join in play fights with wooden swords and plastic axes. Also, if Adrian is defined by testosterone why does he have such individual interests in dance, music and fine art, and a propensity, aside from the occasional play fight with his sisters, to enjoy largely sedentary pastimes?

Adrian's best friend, David, is much more active. He shares Adrian's love of computer role-playing games, but also spends time playing in a rugby team, climbing, abseiling, canoeing and swimming. That doesn't make David any more testosterone driven than his friend. It simply makes David another unique person growing up as an individual within a particular physical body and a particular cultural context.

- Testosterone is one of an infinite number of influences in the lives of boys, but it is not their master.
- Boys will be individuals; time spent learning to live by consent with William, John, Harry and Max is ultimately the best parenting that we can give.

Different Kids

Of course it isn't only boys who suffer from being stereotyped and not engaged with as full, free human beings. If we can avoid relating to our children as mere examples of gender-determined groups there still await other labeling devices that entice us not to relate to children individually. There is a burgeoning plethora of 'diagnoses' that often serve as obstacles to nurturing children as individuals. This is particularly the case with hyperactivity disorders such as ADHD (Attention Deficit Hyperactivity Disorder) or the increasingly popular ODD 'Oppositional Defiance Disorder.' We surely have to wonder how culturally conditioned some diagnoses are when a child opposing the will of adults becomes a recognized affliction or disease for increasing numbers of children.

The problem for parents is often that society is highly judgmental about what meets the criteria of a 'normal' or 'successful' child. Faced with the prospect that their child is not fitting these rigid definitions, parents often feel judged and, in their anxiety, will sometimes go to great lengths to find ways of not being blamed for the faulty-product. Sadly, this doesn't lead to creative thinking, but results in the child being re-labeled. Instead of being 'stupid' or 'clumsy' or a 'daydreamer,' scientific sounding, diagnostic labels are given. The label might feel like a relief to parents; their child has an 'illness' that they did not cause and this may result in assistance for their child.

However in many cases, such 'diagnoses' are thinly disguised control tools. Having a tendency to become engrossed in particular subjects to the exclusion of other things is not objectively a bad thing, but when it doesn't fit the school regime of dividing the day up into artificial subjects controlled by bells it is easier to label the child than to change the system. Faced with diagnoses that seem to have scientific and medical currency, it can be easy for parents to succumb, little suspecting that what they are actually being offered is a system of control to re-fashion the child to the context.

There is nothing wrong with offering up observations that might help our children; "If you don't look at people when you're talking you might find that they think you're lying." "If you don't tie your shoe laces or ask someone to help you with them you might have an accident on your bike." This is reasonable and helpful, but it is not reasonable, helpful or necessary to compel a child into making eye contact by placing him in some behavioral modification program or by constantly barraging him with information that he has long since tired of hearing.

The point is to help the individual child live his own life by his own lights in the way that most pleases him, not to mould him into a new set of attributes which seem more functional and pleasing to parents or other adults in authority. The question that we need to ask for children who appear 'different' is the same question that we should apply to all children, "How can I as a parent help my child to do the things he wants with his life in ways that will not impose anyone's agenda but his own, in ways that will not seek to define or control or modify my child against his will?"

Let's return to Adrian. At 14 he is a happy, confident teenager with some specific interests that he is highly motivated to pursue. At 6 it did not look like Adrian's childhood and adolescent life would turn out so happily. In school Adrian was severely bullied. He couldn't play football, wore spectacles, was clumsy and small for his age. In class he found the background noise overwhelming, seemed to find it impossible to follow group instructions, sometimes showed distress when activities that engaged him were abruptly halted and showed signs of not integrating socially. He would sometimes refuse to stand in line on the grounds that he didn't like being touched and jostled and he constantly wriggled and tried to keep space around him in assemblies, which was seen as disruptive behavior.

After one bullying incident, a very unsatisfactory meeting between Adrian's parents and Adrian's the head teacher took place. It was suggested that perhaps Adrian was stressed because of problems at home, a suggestion that Adrian's parents were taken aback by, resisting the offer of family therapy. It was also suggested that Adrian be assessed with a view to a diagnosis of Asperger's Syndrome. After some soul-searching, Adrian's parents decided to withdraw him from school and educate him at home, an increasingly growing educational alternative.

With his father busy running a small holding and his mother working as a sculptor, Adrian had lots of time to develop his own interests and lots of time to learn through conversations. With this style of education, motivated by his own interests and without the pressures of timetables and bells and large groups, Adrian pursued a unique learning path. At 11 he had only just become a fluent reader, but had a vast store of historical and other knowledge garnered from conversation, numerous visits to castles and TV programs. At 14 he is not merely a fluent, but an avid reader, who also enjoys writing complex stories sparked by his love of fantasy and role-playing games. Moreover, Adrian is happy. He shows every sign of being an individual; he likes to pursue interests in depth and not superficially as he would have to do in school in order to cram in the whole curriculum; he likes his own company or time with one or two friends rather than large groups; he still often forgets to tie his shoe laces and has no interest in football. He is no longer often upset or overwhelmed and he is not viewed as odd and out of place.

Of course some children have real medical problems that are part of their unique problems, but I am convinced that only through consensual interactions in which we address unique individuals can we really be of assistance in our children's lives. Sadly, not everyone agrees; Russell Barkley, for instance, is amongst those who are convinced that 'disease' lies at the heart of educational functionality:

> "Within the past several years, however, those of us who study ADHD have begun to clarify its symptoms and causes and have found that it may have a genetic underpinning. We are finding that ADHD ... arises as a developmental failure in the brain circuitry that underlies inhibition and self-control. This loss of self-control in turn impairs other important brain functions crucial for maintaining attention, including the ability to defer immediate rewards for later, greater gain."

Insisting that ADHD is a disease, Barkley goes on to tell us that it is more likely to affect boys and that it is likely to begin between ages three and five, though can start as late as adolescence. Barkley never considers that this 'late onset' might have some cultural basis in the compulsion children experience in the school environment, but goes on to prescribe a combination of Ritalin, antidepressants and therapy.

Although diagnosing and prescribing continue to be common features of many children's lives, there are voices of caution raised. Baughaman considers that there is no objective difference in the behaviors of so called 'normal' and ADHD children. He contends that no real biological, neurological or genetic bases have been found to support ADHD as a disease. (Baughaman, *Still Seeking ADHD*). Thomas Szasz also articulately expresses protest and warning.

> "Belief in ... ADHD... is a manifestation of the adults' annoyance by certain ordinary childhood activities, their efforts to control or eliminate the activities to allay their own discomfort, and the medical profession's willingness to diagnose disturbing childhood behaviors, thus medicalizing and justifying the domestication of children by drugs defined as therapeutic.
> Formerly, quacks had fake cures for real diseases; now, they claim to have real cures for fake diseases". (Chemical Straitjackets for Children by Thomas S. Szasz Copyright 2001, by The Foundation for Economic Education)

Are increasing numbers of children mentally ill or are our systems of parenting and education poor fits for the vast wealth of individual learning styles and creativity that exist in our children?

- Relating to children via a label rather than as unique individuals merely distances us from being able to assist with real problems.
- If we nurture children to pursue their self–fulfillment, the spin-offs for both individual and society at large will be creative and beneficial.
- It is not in anyone's best interests that children should be forced to fit into a homogenous system at any price. It is a tragic waste of real creativity and potential.
- Whilst there are clearly children who have brain damage or medical conditions that necessitate specialist care and support it is also the case that a vast number of children are being diagnosed and even medicated because they behave in ways that are inconvenient to adults.
- Freed from systematic compulsion these children could live in consent seeking families with all the benefits of innovative and reasoned thinking.

Changing How We Think About Children

How we parent ultimately depends on how we view children. If we think that children are born bad or rebellious, that they are closer to nature, that that boys are a separate species enslaved by testosterone or that some children can only be made to fit by being radically altered with therapy or drugs, then we will respond to them according to those assumptions and we will live in self-fulfilling vicious cycles where what we think is what we get. This will be the case not because our assumptions are right, but because observation is such a loaded activity, we always tend to see what we are looking for and in any case we will fail to see how compulsion is causing the damage we observe.

Change comes when we begin to think differently about children:

- Are children bad or simply limited and ordinary, like adults?
- Do we value obedience above the ability to think?
- Is human nature self-destructive or creative?
- Is selfishness really inconsistent with altruism?
- Do we value static, romanticized ideas of what it is to be 'natural' above the unique individuality of our children?

- Does it really help to relate to our children through stereotypical constructs of what it means to be a 'boy' or 'hyperactive' or is it more helpful to simply relate to the individual?

Consent is for all. We can all, parents and children alike, get what we want and that is a very good thing, as I will set out in the next chapter.

5
You Can't Have Too Much of a Good Thing

One of the strongest memes that operates in parenting is the idea that what we like can't be good for us and, conversely, that suffering is character building. Challenging these ideas can transform not only how we parent, but how we live. Concepts like 'drudgery', 'sacrifice'; even outright 'martyrdom' have a long association with parenting, yet despite all of this parental self-surrender, conventional parenting also baulks at the idea of children getting what they want. Somehow we have come to accept that everyone should lose; parents should be sacrificing themselves for their offspring, but none the less should also live with the gnawing fear that if children get 'too much' of their own way they will turn out to be lazy, ill equipped, uncaring, anti-social, spoiled brats. There is a fundamental assumption that no-one should get too happy or else disaster will ensue, but will it?

No, it won't, because children are:

- Limited, not bad.
- Reasonable and resourceful.
- Full human beings in their own right.

Moreover, we also need to move away from the notion that morality and selfishness are opposites; they are not.

Do What You Want

The win-win mentality doesn't come easily. Parents fear that children who get what they want will turn into intransigent, selfish monsters or become incapable of empathy or altruism. We fear this because for so long we have been told that selfishness and morality are opposites. We are accustomed to thinking about parenting as being about controlling wants and behavior rather than in terms of facilitating wants. Yet if we begin to question the assumptions that children are born uncivilized and that their wants will inevitably be bad for themselves and for others, then such fear makes no sense. Consent-based parenting assumes that being 'self-centered' and doing the moral thing can co-exist. The goal of parenting is not to control, but to help children to follow their inner wishes; to assist them to be the people they want to be for themselves. If children are reasonable, creative, trustworthy, complete human beings living in environments where they have sufficient information to be able to make good decisions for themselves by their own lights, why would we need to control them?

Self-interest is simply a way of making sure that the child makes decisions that are the right ones for that particular individual's learning, growth and well-being. If children rely on parental perceptions of what is right for them, there is actually no way of guaranteeing that the individual child's unique self will be best served. This is because the parents are likely to be working on a preconceived agenda of what is best for children in general or making decisions based on their own perceptions of the child. These might be good approximations, but they can never be equal to the child's self-knowledge. Children who are in touch with their own inner motivation and whose self-interest is being helped will experience greater satisfaction from life, greater belief in their own ability to control their lives and an increase in well-being and self-motivation.

No matter how well a parent knows a child and no matter how well meaning we are as parents, we can never get inside our children's minds. When we spend our time as parents guessing at what is best for another person we will often be wrong. Parents do much better to stay within the role of trusted advisor; offering information, best assumptions and alternatives without presuming that in the final analysis we can know best for another person.

Parents are often concerned that if they concede that their children should act out of self-interest, they will be encouraging their children to become monsters who act immorally and with no regard for other people. Acting out of self-interest is not tantamount to acting badly, nor is it a license for abusive behavior. Doing the best thing for oneself includes doing the right thing. Where it appears to someone that this is not the case, then it is reason and not compulsion that is our best tool in convincing the protagonist otherwise. We can't, ultimately, force someone to lead a moral life, but we can convince children by reason that a moral life and a self-interested life go hand in hand, because the argument will stand up to scrutiny. Immoral acts tend towards not only harming others, but also to being self-destruction on some level. Similarly, it is arguable that harming others is not in anyone's self-interest because it involves giving up one's rights to expect respect and serious treatment in return.

Let's take Russell. At three Russell was already taller and heavier than the other children in his playgroup. Russell lived in a two-parent home with conventional parenting values and although his mother, Anne, was constantly trying to control his behavior she was beginning to feel that she was losing the struggle. At playgroup the other children tried to avoid Russell. The play group leaders were constantly watching him, knowing that any approach he made to another child was likely to result in Russell taking away the toy the other child was playing with, usually with a hard thump thrown in. Everyone was constantly telling Russell 'No!' and he spent lots of time at playgroup sitting alone on the 'naughty chair,' feeling angry and unhappy. Still Russell kept up his belligerent behavior; he had worked out that there were winners and losers and sometimes his strategy for winning worked; with twenty two children in the group he couldn't be watched all the time.

As a rising five year old at school Russell discovered that his strategy for winning was even more useful. Now there were more children and only one teacher plus an assistant. There were lots of opportunities at play times to grab snacks off smaller children or spoil their games. Sometimes these other children told tales about him, so he spent a lot of time being talked to by the head teacher; but more and more the other children were scared by Russell. By the age of seven Russell was a real bully with a growing dossier of concerns in his school file, no friends and a constantly embarrassed mother who was at her wits end.

Russell appeared to be already hardened to suggestion and to be stuck in a cycle of hurting and threatening other children. Russell was also a deeply unhappy child. His tactic of getting his way by force had isolated him. His bullying, far from being an act of self-interest had turned out to be an act of self-destruction. Russell wasn't a winner after all and that was confirmed for him when he graduated to the next school where the older children were bigger and stronger than him. One day in the playground Russell wrestled a skipping rope off an eight-year-old girl, pushing her over and leaving her leg badly grazed. The girl didn't tell the teachers, but went instead to her eleven year old brother and his friends, who decided to take their own action against Russell, laying in wait for him after school.

The next day Anne kept her bruised and shaken child at home and complained to the head teacher, who duly had a stern talk with Russell's attackers and banned them from play ground activities for a week, but the head teacher had a sneaking feeling that Russell had got what he deserved and the boys had a sneaking feeling that their punishment was a token gesture. Anne had the same feeling: no-one as going to go out of their way to protect her son.

Immoral actions don't result in happy, self-fulfilled people, but acts of generosity and service can be acts of self-interest without any contradiction. An aid worker in a famine may give up the prospect of home comforts and put herself into a situation of danger from a desire to effect change and live an altruistic life. Unless she is living her life based on notions of self-destructive irrationality, she will also experience enormous job satisfactions that are in line with her own self-interest.

Parents have no good reason to fear self-interest or to oppose it to morality. Within a family, of course, there will be a collection of self-interested individuals. It is often assumed that one person following their self-interest will inevitably lead to others having to surrender their self-interest. It is a common, but false, characterization of such situations that it will be the parents who are the losers in consensual households. This is not the case! So, why should a child who can have what she wants be interested in helping other family members to get what they want? Isn't the best we can hope for a compromise that people can live with? Isn't the self-interested child going to take up an intransigent stance and repeat his position or demands until they are met, in the full knowledge that he is not going to be compelled?

It is important to stress that mutual agreements are not compromises. If there is a compromise, then it is likely that someone is feeling compelled and someone's self interest has been disregarded. If a child appears intransigent, then perhaps he is unconvinced that it is safe to let go of his original preference and explore new ideas that might bring him something that he prefers even more. Alternatively, he may have already reached a good solution and be genuinely unconvinced by other suggestions. A mutual solution is reached only when every one of the participants genuinely prefers the solution. If every one genuinely prefers something, there is no conflict with self-interest. Children are interested in helping the whole family, parents and siblings, to reach such mutual solutions when they can trust that, in the process, they will be fully respected. Moreover, they will quickly realize that by taking part in finding solutions for everyone they may very well find something that they prefer over their original suggestion. If a child knows that she will not be compelled, there is no reason to cling to a demand without the possibility of thinking or problem solving. After all, it is quite possible that her first suggestion will end up being preferable to everyone and, if not, it will be because she has happily changed her mind herself.

We can get what we want: both parents and children, but doing so relies on building the 'win-win' mentality into our families. Sadly, few of us believe that everyone can win. We are schooled to accept that only some can win, that we must compromise, that we have to take turns at getting what we want. We think like this because we fail to use our resourcefulness and reason. If we are determined to work together to find mutual solutions, it can be done; the more we do it, the more creative we get and the more new ideas we will generate.

Being able to find mutual solutions relies on distinguishing between two important assumptions. The first is that we are limited. Since we are limited, we will make mistakes and we will sometimes fail to find solutions. At any given time, we can only work with the best ideas that we have at that time. Sometimes our ideas are inadequate to the situation, resulting in a dead end, self surrender, or even the use of compulsion. Getting it wrong is part of the human condition and it is going to happen to us whatever form of parenting we follow. Getting it wrong does not mean, however, that no solution was possible, only that we didn't manage to find one on this occasion.

The second thing we must remember as we build a win-win household is simply that there is always, in theory, a solution. We may fail to find solutions because we're human and our ideas are sometimes limited, but this is not the same as believing that no solution was even theoretically possible. There was a solution, probably several solutions, and next time we could find one. This is a very different attitude than the one taken by conventional parenting, which all too often veers between advising parents to put themselves last and self-sacrifice or claims that sometimes children have to be forced to do things. Consent based living proposes a very different fundamental premise; solutions always exist, at least in theory, whether or not we manage to find them in any given situation. This gives us a great basis for building a win-win family ethos. If you don't even think that a solution or an alternative way of doing things is possible then you are hardly going to devote much time and thought to find it.

Let's take the Phorbes family. Eleven-year-old Sally has recently taken up the trumpet. She is so far showing more enthusiasm than promise and the family is not too enamored by the 'music' issuing from her bedroom. Mum, Lisa, and Dad, Stuart are, however, not especially bothered by the sounds and Sally's five year old brother, Freddie, is amused and awed by the instrument. Fourteen-year-old Daniel, though, is reacting much more negatively. Daniel likes quiet. He spends hours reading or painting and has always found a lot of noise or activity overwhelming. Daniel has the quietest room in the house, situated over Stuart's study, but the trumpet noise is causing a lot of conflict between Sally and Daniel.

Daniel says that Sally should practice in the garden shed, but Sally doesn't want to be confined to a cold, cramped space outside and retorts that Daniel should go and read in the shed when she wants to play. Lisa suggests that Sally practice at times when Daniel is not around; when he is at art class or chess club, for instance, but Sally objects that this isn't enough time and anyway she wants to be able to practice when she feels like it and not have to stick to set times. After several ideas have been rejected and everyone is feeling stuck, Stuart returns to the idea of the shed. What if it was cleared out and decorated as a special den, furnished with a portable heater? The idea of a special place tucked away from the house is more appealing to Sally and she begins to join in with the plans.

- Self-interest is not immoral; it is both efficient and good.
- Being self-centered, knowing what you want in life and working out how to achieve it is neither wrong nor inherently opposed to altruism.
- We can all get what we want if we work on building a win-win ethos in our families.
- Solutions exist: not as something fixed and pre-determined that we must mystically divine, but as theoretical possibilities which we discover by innovative thinking.
- What sometimes prevents us finding solutions is not that they can't exist, but simply that we are limited.

If You Like It, It Can Be Good For You

Contrary to popular assumptions, having your preferences met is good, even if you are a child. Even thinking this can evoke all kinds of images of spoilt brats. There often seems to be something immoral or decadent about the suggestion of such satisfaction. We may assume that it entails constant and insatiable material consumption, but none of this need be the case. A spoilt child is a child in distress who is actually never satisfied, whereas self-fulfilling children can be satisfied; the insatiable consumer is a child who is hungering for something that has never been met or identified, not a child who is genuinely getting what she wants. Consent seeking parents don't have to be rich; they simply have to be committed to finding solutions that work for everyone in their particular family. (A theme to which we will return in chapter 10)

Hayley, for example, comes from a family that is incredibly busy and materially well off. Her father, Ramesh, is an executive in a Public Relations company and works long hours. In the little spare time he has available he is intent on keeping fit and, although he loves his eleven-year-old daughter, he has very limited time to give her. Hayley's mother, Kate, is also a very busy person. She runs her own interior decorating company and is very involved in local community activities. Hayley wants for nothing materially and lots of her friends envy her toys and clothes and access to every new CD and DVD. Hayley, it seems, can demand and get anything, but having everything is not actually the same as getting what you want.

Hayley is not happy. She has plenty of material possessions, but not enough fun. Kate notices that almost as soon as Hayley has a new toy or item of clothing or computer game she is bored with it. In fact, Hayley often complains of boredom and 'having nothing to do' and, although Kate has no problem with the amount of money she spends on Hayley's endless lists of wants, she does worry that her daughter appears to be so ungrateful, no matter how much she gives her. She is also concerned that Hayley is so moody, sullen and difficult to please. Unfortunately, worrying is as far as Kate ever seems to get in solving Hayley's problems; she has a business to run and, although she doesn't say so, she resents her daughter's ingratitude. Kate grew up with so much less; she has worked hard all her life and here is Hayley, given the world on a plate and it's never enough.

What Hayley knows, even if she can't articulate it, and what Kate and Ramesh can't admit, is that Hayley is being bought off. The constant gifts are not solutions to problems, but merely the cost of replacing engaged parenting with a rather lavishly veneered neglect. No one in this family is finding mutual solutions. The process of finding mutual solutions enables children to think very clearly through how to achieve goals and set their own priorities. Whether we are rich, poor or somewhere in between we all have choices and finding creative ways of getting wants met rather than merely doling out goods in lieu of resourcefulness is both liberating and a source of learning for everyone involved.

Seeking consent pre-supposes that a child getting what he wants is a very good thing, but this does not mean simply 'giving way' and immediately acquiescing to every proposal. In fact, to simply do this is more likely to result in self surrender or neglect than in satisfied people. If we do not take the time to find genuine solutions with our children then we rob them of the model of reason and innovation that is at the core of consensual parenting and at the core of building a model of getting what we want throughout life. Finding mutual solutions, not doing the first thing that some family member suggests, is the goal. This doesn't mean rejecting an idea just because it's the first one; everyone might love it, but mutual consent, not insatiable material consumption, is the aim.

Suppose Hayley's family decides that finding consent is a better way of living together. One day over breakfast Hayley announces that she wants to change her whole wardrobe. She's tired of jeans and designer tops, and for her twelfth birthday she wants a complete new look; something more individual, probably involving a lot of silk and velvet. Hayley has some fashion magazines with examples and even Kate flinches at the prices of items, especially as she thinks the clothes are likely to be discarded very soon. Inspired by her new consent seeking approach, Kate suggests that perhaps she and Hayley could make some clothes together. Kate is an accomplished craftswoman, though she has never previously taken the time to share her skills and passions with Hayley. Hayley is a little skeptical. She suspects that even if Kate makes enough time to shop for the fabrics with her, she will never get round to actually completing the project. Kate tells Hayley that this would have been true in the past, but she is really serious about making some changes and this leads to a discussion about family time. Kate agrees that if she is really going to nurture her daughter's autonomy she has to make some choices. Her business is going well, she has able staff and she could easily cut back her own workload. In the past she has simply never wanted to, preferring to always be in control and preferring not to spend too much time in Hayley's sullen company. Treating Hayley as a serious individual is going to affect their whole lifestyle and Hayley for one is delighted.

Material possessions in themselves are not bad, but neither are they short cuts for parental involvement. Like many parents who begin the journey of consent seeking, you may have doubts; surely children do have a tendency to prefer things that really do them no good at all. Even given the process of finding mutual solutions, what are we to do if our children want to eat endless sweets or play violent computer games for twelve hours straight or watch horror movies? Surely many things that people like are bad for them and when the people involved are our own children we have a duty to protect them from themselves? I will to return in detail to the issue of acting in our children's best interests in chapter 6 and to the theme of activities that are considered to be bad for children in chapters 8 and 9, but the short answer is that compulsion and impeding our children's wishes are much more 'harmful' for them than a bowl of sweets or a week in front of a computer screen can ever be. The short answer is that children who are treated as reasonable, creative and independent don't have any interest in harming themselves. If an activity is genuinely likely to result in their harm then such children will be open to finding other ways of going about things to get what they want.

- Enjoyment is not a sign of decadence; we learn most and function best when we are having fun and feeling happy.
- Getting what we want isn't merely about ticking off lists of material possessions.
- Spoiled children are children in states of distress who are not having their real wishes met.

- There is nothing wrong with wanting and having 'things', but the most important thing is to use our resourcefulness to find mutual solutions.

Gain Without Pain

Suffering is not all it's cracked up to be and neither is it inevitable, but, goes out the cry, how soft will these children be? The concern is that children who get what they want will have a hard time as adults. People imagine that such children will not be prepared to work for things, but rather will want life handed to them on a plate. Such fear is unfounded; finding mutual solutions is a highly creative endeavor demanding a lot of flexible thinking and a constant flow of new ideas. Getting what we want is not about being handed it, but about engaging creatively with a problem to make sure that what we want happens. Children who are used to finding consent will be more likely to expect to work for things, knowing that creative problem solving is worthwhile and that they can achieve their goals.

It is not uncommon to come across the idea that we need to experience a certain level of frustration, hardship and suffering in order to survive in the real world. What is often forgotten in such insistence is that we all live in the real world. Our circumstance may differ dramatically, but there is still only one world in which we all live. Living well is not 'unreal'. Parents who want to impose some frustration on their children are generally motivated to do so not out of cruelty, but out of fear that otherwise their children will unprepared for whatever life holds, but this is not the case. The argument for deliberately frustrating our children or sometimes purposefully setting out to 'show' them that they can't always 'have their own way' is very similar to the argument for natural consequences and is similarly flawed (as I'll explore further in chapter 6). When parents frustrate their children they are choosing to do so. The hurt is not inevitable, but imposed and artificial. We don't prepare for a journey to a famine-stricken country by starving ourselves, but by building up our strength and learning all we can about basic nutrition and survival.

Let's take Sam and Alfie. It's a sunny summer day and both eight-year-old boys have gone to a rope and wire adventure-climbing course with their families. Sam is with his Dad, Chris and twelve year old sister Leah. Alfie is with his Dad, Ray. The first activity involves climbing up inside a thirty-foot tower and completing a circuit around wires and logs up in the air, attached to a safety harness. The instructor encourages and demonstrates, but is very respectful of what people want to do on the course. Leah confidently completes the course, but her Dad and Sam decide to give this a miss. Ray is also nervous of heading out onto the wire, but he is determined that Alfie should have a go. Ray tells Alfie he's soft and points out that if a girl can get round then he should be able to. Feeling humiliated, Alfie sets out. Although he is held by a harness, the drop looks terrifying, but all the way round Alfie can hear his Dad telling him to be a big boy, telling him not to be a girl, barking orders and sneering whenever Alfie hesitates. By the time Alfie gets round the course he is shaken and upset.

On the climbing wall, Alfie can hear Leah and Chris gently encouraging Sam as he attempts to find hand and foot holds. Sam climbs about half way and his family is just as supportive when he wants to stop as when he wants to go on. Meanwhile, Ray roughly urges Alfie on. Alfie desperately wants to stop, but he is more afraid of his father's scathing response than he is of the wall that stretches above him. Alfie makes it up to the top of the wall and abseils down, but breaks into tears as he lands. Ray is furious and loudly tells Alfie to grow up and stop being a baby. At this point the instructor takes Ray aside and explains that between the pressure to perform and the adrenalin rush of completing the wall, Alfie may need some time and space to compose himself, but Ray isn't about to give Alfie any such space and keeps up the pressure and humiliation all the way round the course.

At the end, Ray slaps his distressed son heartily on the back and says, 'At least you got your money's worth and didn't let a girl beat you, son!' looking pointedly at Sam, who has dabbled with the equipment and had fun. Alfie, however, isn't feeling so triumphant. He throws his helmet to the floor, shouting that he never wants to go anywhere with his Dad again and runs to the car, crying. Meanwhile Sam tells Chris and Leah that next time he thinks he'll be able to do more of the activities because now he knows what they are about and he has enjoyed watching Leah safely complete things without any pressure on him to do the same. Once again the instructor goes over to Alfie to encourage and comfort him and when Ray joins them the instructor suggests that on future occasions it might be best not to put so much pressure on Alfie, to which Ray retorts, 'I had no choice! Someone has to teach him to be a man.'

Alfie never returns to the climbing course, but Sam visits again and completes a little bit more each time, setting himself goals and rising to challenges without any fear of humiliation or rejection from his family.

- Life contains enough risks and enough learning opportunities for children to see for themselves that bad things happen.

- Children can learn how to tackle and handle the real tragedies and complex problems of life by having lots of access to information, by having good models of how to creatively problem solve and by simply living.
- There is no intrinsic value in being in a state of suffering or distress; it only serves to crush our ability to think reasonably and creatively.

No-one Has to Lose

A win-win ethos is commonly hampered by the belief that someone has to lose, but why should this be so? Despite our limitations, the conviction that solutions are possible and the use of our resourcefulness go a very long way. Children can get what they want, but that doesn't have to be at their parents' expense. Consent based living is about everyone getting his or her own way. There is no need to demonize self-interest and children getting what they want, but neither do we need to promote parental self-surrender. We all get what we want when we find a mutual solution. Of course we are limited and when we fail it is preferable not to compel, so this may mean that the parent, in this instance doesn't get what he wants. This is not ideal or recommended, but a human default when our resourcefulness fails us. It shouldn't become a pattern and it should become an increasingly infrequently used default as we get better and better at finding mutual solutions. Sadly, many of us who have had a life time of compulsion and carry around ingrained ideas that make it hard for us to change our own minds and so we sometimes end up self-sacrificing. There is no magic for implementing consent in our families and we will be constantly exposing new layers of compulsion and new areas in which we have a lot to learn, but consensual parenting is not a theory of self-surrender; the goal is for everyone to get what they want and once this really sinks in it is enormously liberating.

Conventional parenting polarizes families. On one side there are parents, struggling to retain control and impose boundaries that are deemed to be in the children's best interests. On the other side are children, working towards opposite ends, unless the parents take over the reins and steer the family to the good. Without 'loving discipline', the wisdom runs, children will become selfish, insatiable monsters. The notion of artificial boundaries, aided by the myth that we can't all win and that there must be compromises and losers prevents consent being achieved. We need to reject these assumptions. In consent based families everyone is expected to be on their own side. Each individual knows best what he or she wants and prefers. Far from creating untold conflict, this allows for reasonable discussion of how all of these interests can be met through mutual solutions where everyone wins. There is no such thing as doing something in the 'family's best interest' when one or more members of the family are deeply unhappy with the solution.

Being able to create an environment in which everyone wins relies on several things. It is absolutely necessary that children can trust that they can enter into the process of finding mutual solutions without fear of compulsion. It is only when they can do this that they will be able to see that changing their preferences is compatible with achieving what they want. Without this trust, they are much more likely to rigidly stick to their first preference, fearing that if they show any open-mindedness on a particular subject they will merely be trampled upon. Similarly, parents must be willing to enter into the process of finding solutions without having already decided what the outcome must be. They must be willing not simply to desist from compulsion, but also to use all their resourcefulness to find mutual solutions. So, parents and children are not working against one another, but are working for consent and mutual solution. What might this look like?

Meet the Smith-Bowler family. The family consists of Laura and her partner, Hannah, with children Molly (13), Nick (10) and Toby (6). Laura works in a busy inner city community center as a counselor and family worker. Over the past few years she has been increasingly dissatisfied with her long hours, low pay and high stress. She secretly wants to be a full time potter, but a city mortgage and lifestyle leave her little time and little spare money. Hannah teaches yoga part time, taking classes at nearby leisure centers. She would like to work more, but the market seems to be saturated in her area. Laura and Hannah have a big mortgage because houses in their city are expensive and this leaves less money for family activities than everyone would like. Thirteen-year-old Molly loves living in the city. She has plenty of friends, likes to shop and loves going to the cinema. Unfortunately, there never seems to be enough money for her to join in all the things her friends do or to buy as many clothes, as much make-up and keep up with all the new music and videos. Molly also wants a new computer, but that is out of reach at the moment. Nick is an active boy who plays football at a local club and does karate and swimming lessons at the local sports center. He would like to learn more sports; he wants to learn to canoe and go white water rafting and he wants to do a course in climbing and abseiling. These things are expensive, especially in a city. Nick secretly longs to live in the country and have his own bedroom, apart from Toby, but he doesn't see these things ever happening. Toby is a contented six year old, but he wishes Nick wouldn't constantly get so cross whenever he so much as lays a finger on his brother's stuff, which is always lying about their bedroom. Toby would love to have a dog, but Laura and Hannah say that the city is no place for dogs and they don't have the time to walk it or the money to care for it.

Most days the Smith-Bowlers get on with their lives; they are busy, caring people, who like each other, but sometimes their secret wishes and frustrations gnaw at them and the atmosphere becomes tense. Well, that's life; or is it?

After a really stressful period at work, Laura gets a heavy head cold and decides she has to take some time off. She soon realizes that after only a week at home, a week when she hadn't even been feeling her best, she feels so much more relaxed and happy and the whole mood of the house is better. She's had more time to sit around with Molly and listen to music and more time to snuggle up with Toby and his favorite picture books. She even enjoyed going out on Saturday morning to watch Nick play football, instead of feeling her usual resentful self and worrying about all the housework that wasn't being done. If only she didn't have to return to this job that she used to love, but now is stifling and overwhelming her. Back at work, Laura discovers some websites on living by consent whilst searching for some family support sites for a client. She is fascinated and over the next few weeks she and Hannah join a support list and spend a lot of time talking and thinking about consent based parenting.

Despite having lots of questions and doubts, Laura and Hannah begin to parent with mutual solutions in mind and the family seems happier and more relaxed. With more creative thinking Molly notices that she gets to do more of the things that she wants; the family is not richer, but somehow Laura and Hannah are able to think more resourcefully, prioritize differently and take Molly's wishes on board. Feeling that she is being treated as a serious individual, Molly feels less belligerent when she can't buy the whole video store and more willing to work with Laura and Hannah to find solutions. Nick goes on a climbing course, but it's just a short taster and he wishes he could have more. He likes the idea that everyone can get what they want, but doesn't mention his wish to live in the country in a bigger house; he's not that optimistic. After a lot of resistance Toby gets his dog, though not without some self-surrender from Laura and Hannah. They take turns to go with Toby on walks that neither of them enjoys and Molly isn't too keen on the dog, which she complains is going to get too big for their three bed-roomed city house. When the largest local leisure center closes for refurbishment a few months later, Hannah loses one of her main sources of income and the family's newfound resourcefulness looks to be under serious threat.

Working with their new consent seeking assumptions, the Smith-Bowlers decide to take a look at their life. In the new atmosphere of trust Laura tells the others about her dream of leaving work to become a potter, her long-term hobby. Encouraged by this revelation Nick says he wishes that they could move out of the city and Toby agrees that he and Jet (the dog) would also like this. Molly says that no way is she leaving the city and her friends and Hannah agrees that she likes city life, though she is very worried about not having enough work in their area. Laura has never really thought about moving before, she has always assumed that her job and the house were fixed burdens, but now she begins to question this. She begins by addressing Molly's worries. What if they could find a country house near a reasonably sized town? What if the move released some capital so that Molly could have a computer with broadband connection so that Molly could keep in touch with friends? What if Molly could make regular trips to stay with friends and invite them to stay with her? What if they could find a house with a bigger room for Molly to decorate, as she wanted, instead of the smallest room in the house that she is currently squeezed into? Despite her initial reservations, Molly is willing to give the idea some thought and later joins Laura and Hannah at the library to do an Internet search for where the cheaper country areas are.

A year after hearing about consensual parenting the Smith-Bowlers lives look quite different. They are living in a village on the end of a terrace of two hundred and fifty year old houses, in a house that cost half of what their city home sold for, even though it has four bedrooms and stunning views. At fourteen, Molly can travel on the train back to the city to visit friends and speaks to many of them most evenings in chat rooms using her new computer in her new, bigger purple bedroom. Nick loves all the outdoor pursuits available and he and Hannah have bought their own canoe. Toby can safely take Jet for walks by himself around the quiet little village, although Laura and Hannah often choose to go with him, because the local walks are so relaxing. Laura is a potter. She has a tiny, but adequate workshop in a converted outdoor toilet block at the end of their garden, fitted with a new wheel and second hand kiln. Slowly, she is finding outlets in local craft galleries for her work. She isn't making nearly as much money as she was in her city job, which she always considered underpaid, but she has no costs of getting to work, no smart work clothes to buy, has time to cook instead of buying expensive convenience foods and a much smaller mortgage to contribute to. Hannah, on the other hand, has found much more work than she did in the city with fewer yoga teachers to compete with in their new locality.

The important thing is that a solution is found which everyone generally prefers. There are many ways of problem solving, as many as our joint resourcefulness allows. Sometimes a useful way to problem solve is to take apart the expressed preferences and see what are the elements that are making something a want. For example, when Kyle says he wants to go to the local Scouts group, but then objects that he hates all the lining up and orders, perhaps the family can look a little more closely at what exactly Kyle wanted from the Scout group. Does he like camping trips? Does he want a regular group of friends to play games with? Does he like the singing session? What exactly is Kyle looking for and what are the other ways that these wants can be met?

When Jane wants to go ice-skating, Philip wants to go to the movies and Ellie wants to go to the park, no one seems to be open-minded until Mum says, 'How about a trip to Disneyland instead?' Suddenly, everyone is in agreement. It doesn't have to be Disneyland. The point is that most families have a few activities that they really enjoy and which can be used to break an impasse. It might be that the solution needed is something that isn't amongst any of the initial preferences, but something entirely different; something that doesn't have the feel of one person being talked into doing another person's choice but, instead, enables everyone to think outside of the current box.

If children trust that they will not be risking compulsion by taking part in problem solving, if their resourcefulness is valued and used, then the idea of changing preferences becomes much less threatening. Parents can generally see that the ability of children to change their minds is a crucial one, but it is much easier to overlook the necessity for adults to change their preferences too. In chapter one I looked at how compulsion damages our ability to think and at how we can develop deeply fixed ideas. This can happen to anyone, at any age, but adults have generally encountered much more compulsion damage and are particularly likely to have areas that they find it virtually impossible to discuss clearly and openly. Parents too must be willing to change their preferences, if they are to help to make consent become the way their family operates.

Changing our preferences is not the same as self-surrender. If we are looking for genuine consent and mutual solutions, the changes in our thinking have to be real. If we feel that we are merely compromising, or if we feel resentful or uneasy about solutions, then there is no point in kidding ourselves that we have arrived at a mutual solution. Changing preferences isn't easy, especially in those areas where our thinking has always been very fixed, but the more we commit ourselves to finding consent and the more we practice finding mutual solutions, the more it will happen. One thing that we can do to help the process is to ask ourselves if the thing we are expressing a preference about is really an area where we have the right to interfere. I might prefer a tidy house, but does that give me a right to insist that my children should have tidy bedrooms any more than I would have the right to insist that an adult friend should have a tidy house? I might prefer a vegetarian diet, but does that give me the right to impose a vegetarian diet on my children?

I am not suggesting that these (or any other areas) are simple or clear-cut. The examples above are complicated by the fact that we have a special relationship with our children, and they might be happy to reach a mutual solution with us even if we don't have a 'right' to expect this. The examples are also complicated by the practicalities of sharing a home, and by the fact that we have a responsibility as parents to share information and our best ideas about hygiene and life-style and diet and anything else. However, even with these provisos, it can sometimes help us to see things differently if we simply ask ourselves, 'Would I presume to interfere so closely with an adult friend? Is this properly an area where I should be expressing a preference?'

Another way in which we can help ourselves to change preferences is to seek criticism of our ideas and keep looking for new information. Children can be our most astute and valuable critics. If they trust that it is safe to do so, they will generally be very generous with their views, pointing out compulsion and presenting cogent reasons why our pet ideas might be wrong after all. More widely, there are other people trying to live consensually, and gaining access to their ideas can be an invaluable aid in working on the ideas we find most difficult to let go of. It might be through mailing lists or blogs, through accessing advice and support or through building relationships with particular families.

In addition to asking ourselves whether we are overstepping personal boundaries or seeking criticism of our ideas, a third way of helping ourselves to change preferences is to ask ourselves what we care about most. Are we really more wedded to an idea that watching more than two hours of TV is bad for a person than we are to our child's happiness? Do we really think that avoiding a glass of cola is more important to our child's well being and thinking than avoiding massive distress? Consent based living is not a burdensome code to be slavishly followed and implemented, but a positive choice about how we value one another and want to behave morally and creatively towards one another. Simply reminding ourselves of this can often help us to begin solving problems that seem to have come to an impasse.

At other times, we may simply need more time. An idea may be so entrenched that we are not ready to examine it yet. We may need more practice at finding mutual solutions in easier areas before we are willing to return to difficult ground. At such times, the best thing we can do is to back off. There are plenty of other problems to be solved.

- There are no rules for finding mutual solutions. What works for one family may be of little use to another.
- Believing that a solution is possible, even if we don't find it, is a major part of the process.
- It is important that the participants believe themselves to be on the same side, rather than seeing themselves as adversaries.
- Everyone must be able to discuss their preferences openly, teasing out the vital elements of a preference that may lead to new solutions, and being able to risk changing their minds without fear of compulsion.
- Creativity and self-interest must be fully valued and utilized.
- The process of finding mutual solutions flourishes when concepts such as fairness are abandoned.

Without Fairness

Parenting needs to stop falling back on the idea of fairness. Fairness is a meme that limits how often a child can win, introduces turn taking into the notion of getting preferences met and ultimately fails, causing as much resentment as it was ever meant to avoid. The myth of 'fairness' often stands in the way of finding mutual solution.

Conventional parenting tells us that all children should be treated the same or equally. If we buy Lizzie a bar of chocolate we should get an identical bar for Joe. If we spend an hour reading to Joe, we should spend the next hour drawing with Lizzie. Most of us were brought up in families where parents and grandparents told us, 'You can't give to one without giving to the other.' Surely, it is common sense that we should treat our children fairly and equally, that we shouldn't discriminate between them? Children are individuals. If we buy Joe chocolate simply because we bought some for Lizzie, we are not taking any notice of Joe's individuality and real preferences, we are merely relating to him by means of a mechanical principle.

The notion of fairness promotes a climate of sibling rivalry in which children are constantly watching one another and their parents for signals of unfairness or favor. Conversely, if we treat each child as a unique individual with his or her own preferences which we want to help them achieve, then both fairness and rivalry become superfluous. Lizzie wants chocolate and a movie. Joe wants to spend some time reading with mum and would like pizza for tea. Perhaps all of those things are simply achievable. Perhaps there is some problem. The answer isn't to tell Joe, 'Well, today we are all going to the movies. I'll buy you some sweets and I'm sure you'll enjoy it, really. I read to you yesterday. So it's only fair.' The answer is to find a mutual solution. That may mean that everyone will do the same thing because everyone decides that they hadn't considered the idea of going bowling and they'd all prefer that to their original ideas. It may mean Lizzie will end up going for a bike ride with her friend and stopping off at the sweet shop on her way, whilst Mum and Joe snuggle up with the book and later Dad cooks paella, which everyone prefers to pizza. When we treat each child as a unique and independent person, we have to abandon any allegiance to mechanical rules.

- Don't treat your children fairly; treat them as unique individuals.

6
In the Name of Love

Children are children; they lack experience and the wisdom of age. Parents have been there, done that, got the t-shirt and sometimes the scars to prove it, so surely there are boundaries that parents need to set in the name of love and their children's best interests. No?

Not Because I Say So

All other arguments aside, many people believe that children simply owe love and obedience to parents by dint of their role. What parent hasn't uttered the words 'do as you're told, because I say so'? And why shouldn't we? We shouldn't because the meme is false. As I've said before, obedience is a dangerous parenting tool; you may not think that having a highly biddable child is quite so convenient when the bidding is coming from the local drug dealer. The call for obedient children can take two forms: one is that children are born with a propensity to do the wrong thing and therefore these 'fallen' children need to be directed, the other is that adults are natural authority figures in the lives of children. These beliefs are so widespread that they have taken on the appearance of being obvious, but as consent-seeking parents, we are in the business of questioning everything.

Some parents see their parental authority as a delegation of divine authority along a hierarchical chain. Holding religious views and living by consent are certainly compatible, but forcing one's own religious beliefs onto a child is not. If a parent believes in divine authority, he should share his ideas with his children fully, but stop short of forcing his views onto them.

For others authority is linked to some kind of contract. Some people think of families as similar to democratic countries. Democracy works because the participants recognize the rule of law as the best political theory we have so far devised. The authority holds while the government remains democratic and responsive and whilst the law is seen to be just and rational. The authority fails when people lose confidence in the rule of law through corruption or injustice. However, families are not like countries. Our children do not have a contract with us; they did not consent to be born and did not elect us as their parents. Societal systems are means of dealing with the problems of large scale interactions, but families, even large families, are much smaller, more personal and parents have direct responsibilities towards their children that are unique to this relationship; no-one but my children can claim that I am directly responsible for their existence.

Other types of authority derive from expertise; we entrust aspects of health care to medical professionals or allow the mechanic to make decisions when our car breaks down. Parents generally come with more experience and more ideas than their children and we would be neglectful not to share this, but the analogy is still limited. In all but the direst emergencies we expect medical professionals to give us information and consult us fully before we give our final informed consent to treatment and procedures. The doctor may have the expertise and we would often be wise to listen to it, but she can't make our decisions for us. We expect the mechanic to have the expertise to fix our car, but we also expect that he will tell us what the problem is, give us a quote for the work and not carry out work without our go ahead. Parents are founts of experience, some of which is very valuable and some less so. Parents are wonderful sources of advice and ideas. Parents are the best resource a child can have, but that doesn't make us absolute authorities with the right to decide how the child should live.

There are some parents for whom authority is a matter of ownership; I have the authority to dispose of my own money and property in whatever way I see fit and this argument is carried over into family relationships with the idea that a parent can do what she wants with her children. We don't own our children! They are not goods, but reasonable, creative, autonomous human beings. They are complete people just like us; they have lived for less time, may have less articulate ideas and less experience, but they do not have less humanity.

In the film *Tea with Mussolini; a story of civilized disobedience,* there is a fictionalized account of real events during the Second World War in Italy. One of the characters is a young boy entrusted to the care of an English governess, Mary Wallace. As his father becomes entangled with Mussolini's fascism, Luca is taken away from the liberal influence of Mary and sent to a Hitler youth school in Austria. Luca, though, has already been 'infected' by Mary's liberal way of thinking for himself about right and wrong and when he returns from the school to find Mary and her English friends in a prisoner of war camp he becomes part of their 'civilized disobedience', even saving the life of a Jewish American woman who has lost everything. The decisions that Luca has to make are complex and clouded by the emotions of adolescent feelings of infatuation and betrayal, as well as confusion about identity and loyalty, but despite all of this, Luca is able to make mature and courageous decisions. Many children of Luca's generation in Italy,

Germany and Austria did not fare so well; brought up on diets of obedience the handover to 'Hitler youth' was a smoother process for them than for Luca.

When your child next asks why he should do something, stop before you say, 'because I'm your father and I say so.' It is a very insufficient argument. If you are actually saying, 'because God says...' then you should set out your belief in such a way that your child can make her own decision about faith. If what you really mean is, 'because it's against the law not to wear seatbelts' then you should be able to find a way of living within your particular context that both you and your child find reasonable and can consent to. If what you mean to say is, 'because I've been in this situation and I know best' then your argument should be able to stand up to scrutiny. If your reasoning makes sense to your child, then arguments from authority are superfluous, if not, then perhaps there is more to the issue or perhaps you need to revise your assumptions. If you are genuinely saying, 'because you are my child, so you'll do as I say', then you are asking for the kind of blind, unreasonable obedience that is going to assist your child in becoming a malleable person, and it won't always be you or anyone with good intentions doing the molding. Now is a good time to re-examine your ideas.

Catharine and Jamaica are two college students away from home for the first time. Catharine comes from a loving, strict home where conformity and obedience is highly valued. Unlike her brother, Joshua, this was never a problem for Catharine. A quiet, academic child, she always wanted to please her parents and teachers. Catharine's parents have protected her all the way through adolescence, defending her from bad influences, limiting her access to TV, controlling her information about sexuality, shielding her from knowledge of drugs and teaching her to be a 'good' girl. Jamaica comes from a very different home; she has been exposed to information and ideas from babyhood. Her consent seeking parents have always shared their ideas on morality with Jamaica and have always been open to Jamaica's criticisms. Whenever Jamaica has a problem or needs to make a decision she always looks to her parents as good sources of information and advice and she always knows that in the final analysis the decision will be hers to make.

Whilst Jamaica thrives at college, within months the problems are piling up for Catharine. Her finances soon run into difficulties; she has never been in control of money before or even been privy to real information about family budgeting. Floundering, she is too worried to contact her parents for advice, fearing their disappointment and disapproval, but that is the least of her problems. Catharine's naivety and over-eagerness to please anyone she meets are like beacons to the unscrupulous and Jamaica is increasingly concerned for her friend as she risks pregnancy, suffers rejections, and becomes embroiled in experimenting with drugs without information or control. A year later, depressed and failing in her course, Catharine is easy prey for a cult group promising Catharine safety and salvation in return for obedience.

- We don't own our children; they are people, not property
- Parents should share information, expertise, morality, theories, assumptions and experience, but should not presume to make decisions for their children.
- Our children have never entered into a contract that grants us authority over them. On the other hand, parents do have special responsibilities towards children.
- Whatever authority we might choose to recognize in our own life, we can do no more than fully share our reasons and allow our arguments to stand or fall on their merits by our children's lights.

Not For Your Own Good

There are times when we genuinely believe that we know best and, with the highest of intentions, we are so concerned about our children that any thought of reasonable discussion rushes from our head in the panic to ensure that the right thing is done. Are 'best interests' really a justification for making decisions over the head of another human being?

All parenting has the child's best interests at heart, unless, of course, it is deliberately abusive, but it is not always as simple as it looks to define what might be in the best interests of a particular unique individual at a particular time. That is not to say that the parent does not have an enormous role in giving advice, best ideas and information, but, in the final analysis, best interest must be something that a person judges for himself. As a parent I may have assumptions about right and wrong or diet or sleep that I should share as fully as the child desires; but imposition of those ideas is not an option. Why not? Firstly, because no matter how convinced I am, I could still be wrong. In order to resist the impulse to act in someone else's best interests we have to believe two things; that they are separate, free individuals and that we are limited.

There have been countless ideas held over time that in their day have been held as absolute, indisputable facts, only to be proved totally unfounded a few years later. Nutrition theories are an obvious example; in sixties Britain the nation was advised to 'go to work on an egg', whereas today we are admonished to restrict egg intake to a maximum of three a week. A much more extreme example might be female genital mutilation. According to Amnesty International, this still widely practiced custom comes with its own raft of beliefs about the 'best interests' of girls and women. Amongst the rationale for this practice, which can have devastating physical and psychological effects, are issues of bestowing cultural identity and belonging, of delineating gender identity and beliefs that it is hygienic and aesthetically superior. In cultures where female genital mutilation is practiced there is an overwhelming belief that parents are acting in their children's best interests. This might seem clearly wrong from a Western perspective, but we only have to look as far back as nineteenth century Britain to find the that clitoridectomy was believed to cure hysteria. Those who hold the view that genital mutilation is beneficial think that it is self-evidently so. Absolute belief and a lack of respect for the independence of children are a powerful and dangerous combination.

Of course this is an extreme example, but the harm we do when we use force is not something that we can easily quantify. Since we can't get inside the minds of our children we never really know which acts of compulsion are going to shut down whole areas of learning and enjoyment for them or cause them to have poor ideas in particular areas of their lives. Even when an idea seems absolutely obvious to us, even when we know that we are right, we still could be wrong. What right has one limited human being to compromise the autonomy of another? No matter how well a parent knows their child, and no matter how much they love their child, they are not their child.

Take Paul, for example. His parents have always strictly controlled what he sees on TV and video, but one day, at a relative's house, Paul (aged 9) watches a teenage horror movie with his older cousin, Colin. That night, Paul has terrible nightmares and admits to his mother that he has seen a movie that he has been forbidden to watch. Paul's mother lectures him about how violence gets inside people's minds and about how he is not old enough to see these things, telling him that it's his own fault he is now suffering nightmares. Paul feels scared in bed for nights after the incident, but keeps his fears to himself, not wanting any more lectures.

A couple of months later Paul's friend Sean also mentions seeing the same movie. Sean lives in a consent seeking home and he is able to select his own viewing, with the help of input and conversation. Sean's Mum thinks that the movie is likely to be the kind that will upset Sean and she tells him this. Sean thinks his

Mum might be right, but he wants to be able to join in with his siblings, 15 year old twins Ian and Amy. He also has some ideas about experimenting with his own levels of fear, though these ideas aren't easy for him to articulate. He asks his Mum to watch too. During the movie there are moments when Sean feels like leaving the room, but he also has a strong compulsion to see this through. That night Sean doesn't want to sleep alone and Ian agrees to Sean putting up a camp bed in his room. The next day Sean talks to his Mum constantly about the film and by evening he feels that he will be fine in his own room, but he has nightmares. His Mum comforts him and stays with him till he is asleep again. The next day Sean decides that he will watch the movie again and again and again. By the time he's seen it repeatedly the images begin to lose their power and he feels comfortable again.

Sean's brother, Ian, tells him he used to handle things quite differently when he was nine. Ian also had the freedom to watch what he wanted with lots of information and advice available and support for his decisions. Ian soon developed a very sophisticated screening process that was unique to his own needs. He couldn't have told anyone how he made decisions, but he found that he could always quickly assess whether a movie would be too scary for him and, at Sean's age, he didn't want to feel frightened.

Both boys found quite different ways of coping with potential fear; one welcomed the buzz, but needed help in handling it, the other developed a kind of protective antenna. Sean and Ian did just what adults do; they made decisions by their own lights to suit their own personalities and support networks. It is not always irrational to watch frightening things; it may be a source of learning and fun; what matters is the individual involved rather than a mechanical rule.

- Our best ideas might well be true, but because we are limited we must hold them tentatively and not impose them.
- We should always stop short of compulsion – we don't know what damage we might do and we can never get inside the mind of another individual, even our child.

Love Without Force

If not best interests, then surely love justifies a certain amount of compulsion? Love isn't all sentiment and giving in, after all. Think again: love doesn't justify compulsion and this is why. A child is a separate person with a moral right to his or her own decisions. Love is not a good enough excuse for acting immorally to deliberately compromise another person's selfhood. The idea of loving compulsion is pernicious, and runs through every strand of conventional parenting. Permissive parents inflict damaging neglect in the name of love. 'I wouldn't dream of making suggestions to Terry, it would be so disrespectful.' No, it wouldn't! If you are Terry's Dad then you have a responsibility to share your morality and all of your best ideas with Terry. It is not loving to let your child flounder without information, advice, moral opinion and input.

Authoritarian parents, on the other hand, inflict discipline, from spanking to time out to loss of privileges, in the name of love. 'It hurts me to have to discipline you, but it's for your own good.' 'I'm only taking your pocket money away because I care so much.' Learning is something that takes place in the mind of the child. If your child does something you consider to be immoral you should say so, you should share your arguments fully; you have a responsibility to do so for as long as your child is willing to engage and listen, but you should stop short of inflicting immoral force yourself.

Liberal parents seek to impose firm but loving limits, 'So far and no further.' However, the problem with these loving limits is that not only do artificial boundaries simply beg to be pushed and pushed, but also no two liberal parents ever agree on what they should be. They become a matter of personal preference and relativism. Sandra's parents claim that she can play when she wants, eat what she wants, sleep when she wants, but she must brush her teeth twice a day no matter what. Sunita's parents tell her that is fine to skip tooth brushing sometimes and give her lots of freedom, but are absolutely adamant about regular bed times. Neil's parents are very liberal, except when it comes to anything on a screen; TV and computers, it seems, are of the devil. Why should children be convinced that these are real boundaries that cannot be crossed when no two sets of parents can agree on them? Children may very well be right to suspect that what is being done to them is not about love and their best interests, but more about their parents own areas of entrenched thinking and irrationality.

Consent based living demands a great deal of engagement, but it does not require that we take our children over. Usurping our children's lives is not an act of love, but of desperation; we do it when we have run out of creativity or when our arguments don't bear our children's scrutiny. Living by consent requires that we completely eschew the idea that compulsion of any kind, no matter how subtly conceived and implemented, can be an act of love. Of course consent seeking parents do not have the monopoly on love any more than they do on infallibility. The point is simply that a big shift in perception is needed for consensual parenting to take place; a shift away from the idea that love justifies our compulsion, of whatever form.

- Love is not an excuse for acting immorally.

Forget Consistency

Surely children need structure? They need parents who show a united front to give them a clear moral framework, to make them feel safe and confident. Surely all right-thinking people would agree on that? No. Children need to be treated as full humans and adults need to stop colluding against them.

There is a strong parenting meme that says that it is very important for children to see all the significant adults in their life standing together. This clear united front is supposed to impress on children the rightness of the idea they are being sold at that moment. If Mum and Dad disagree then children might suspect that there are more choices than they are being told about or they might get the dangerous notion that they can play one parent off against the other to 'get their own manipulative way.' If Mum questions the amount of homework a child is given then school authority might come crashing down and destroy the universe as we know it. If Dad questions Mum when she insists on Nigel eating every last scrap of cabbage then the whole edifice of parental collusion will collapse. This meme relies on the hideous idea that children and adults are inevitably at war and that a united front on the part of the adults is the only way to win. When we are living by consent and know that everyone can win, we have no need for such damaging collusion against our children.

Mary lives in a family that sees itself as 'alternative.' There is no TV, a vegan diet, an emphasis on caring for the environment and on not consuming too much of the world's resources. Mary's parents have very clear values by which they live and by which they raise Mary. However, by the age of twelve, Mary is beginning to question some of those values and her politically correct lifestyle is beginning to feel like a straight jacket that prevents her from joining in with many of the activities of her friends. Mary's Dad, Oliver, is also beginning to feel uneasy. He still holds to his values, but he is no longer so comfortable with forcing them wholesale onto Mary.

When she was a small child this seemed easier, but now she is rapidly getting out of step with her peers and although Oliver likes his child to be 'different' he doesn't want her to be isolated and unhappy. He tries to talk to his partner, Naomi, about relaxing the restrictions on Mary, but Naomi is adamant that this would mean 'selling out' and betraying their values and she is also very concerned that she and Oliver should be presenting a united front. She acknowledges that life might be a little difficult for Mary now, but is sure that Mary will thank them for this later when she grows up with strong ideals and beliefs and becomes a caring, socially aware young woman. Naomi insists that Mary is at a very fragile stage of development; if Oliver shows any signs of doubt this will simply confuse Mary and leave her vulnerable to peer pressure and to growing up without any clear moral framework.

Mary is already confused, however. Clearly her friends and most of their parents think quite differently from her own parents. Moreover she senses that her father is not so rock solid in his values and how to pass them on as her mother. Little by little, Mary begins to use this knowledge to plant more doubts in Oliver's mind. Over time she finds that she can get concessions from Oliver if she hides what she is doing from Naomi, building a web of deceit, mistrust and subterfuge that is likely to be a time bomb for family relationships.

Hannah (aged 14) lives in a very different context. During the week she is usually with her mother, Diane, a writer and feminist activist. At weekends she generally stays with her father, Noel, his wife, Joanne and her stepsister, Claire (aged 11). Hannah's family work hard to implement consent in their lives and since they discovered this idea they have been pleasantly surprised at how much tension has evaporated between them. Diane has lots of firm views and she shares these freely with her daughter. Diane only reads novels written by women, eats organic foods, gives lots of time to the local credit union and recycles as much as she possibly can. Noel and Joanne have a rather more mainstream lifestyle. There is always plenty of cola in the fridge; Noel, a cinema critic, loves watching movies with Hannah and Claire and Joanne, a P.A., enjoys taking the girls out clothes shopping.

Before beginning to live in consent seeking ways, Diane was constantly anxious that Hannah was being exposed to all the 'wrong' influences when she stayed with her father and she didn't always appreciate the 'girlie' clothes that Hannah brought home from her shopping trips with Joanne. Now Diane is much more relaxed. She can see that her daughter is able to weigh and sift lots of conflicting information and make her own decisions and draw her own conclusions. She feels much less compelled to interfere in areas of personal preference like make-up and clothes, although Hannah is also much less defensive about hearing Diane's opinions now that she knows they are not loaded with manipulation. Joanne and Noel are also more relaxed. They are much less dismissive of Diane's lifestyle and views now that they feel that they are not being forced onto Hannah and this improved relationship has helped Hannah to join in with finding mutual solutions rather than wanting or needing to play one set of parents off against the other.

Why should we assume that children will become confused and unable to make good decisions simply because they learn that not all adults agree on everything, even when the adults happen to be their parents? Children are not imbeciles. They very quickly acquire the knowledge that there are competing opinions on many subjects, but they don't need to acquire the knowledge that their own parents have been deliberately lying to them about this. Children are quite able to handle a home in which there are competing ideas so long as they are not presented as acts of war. By the same token, the problem of having a child who will 'divide and rule' his parents cannot occur where the whole environment is geared to assisting win-win solutions.

The need for consistency is a by-product of non consensual situations. If Dawn knows that she is going to be compelled, then it is probably easier and less frightening for her to know what the rules are and what might happen to her if she breaks them. Living in a haphazard environment where one day Mum doesn't care if you chalk on the walls and the next day she will smack you hard and scream the house down is not a prospect anyone could relish and it is inevitably scary to a small child. In a consensual environment there is no such need. Consistency and safety comes not from knowing the rules, but from knowing that although Mum thinks its fine to eat meat and Dad thinks its wrong, neither is going to compel you, but rather both will offer their best ideas whilst your right to make a decision will be respected.

- It is wrong and unnecessary to collude against children to show a false united front.
- In a win-win environment the parents and children are all on the same side.
- Consistency and safety are provided better by respecting a child than by rule-setting.

No More 'That'll Teach You'

If we don't give our children rules, many will argue, then they will run into them anyway. Many actions have consequences and the consequences of some behavior can be harsh but realistic teachers. Is this the case or are natural consequences not so natural or so inevitable as we imagine?

Conventional parenting tends to claim that certain bad things happen because they are 'inevitable'. 'If you don't eat up your breakfast, you will suffer from hunger;' 'If you climb in that tree, you will fall and hurt yourself;' 'If you run around the house, you will cause an accident;' 'If you don't go to sleep at a reasonable hour, you will make yourself ill' and so on. Parents can make it look as though the bad thing that happens simply has to happen, but this is simply not true. There are lots of different things that might happen if you avoid breakfast, like having a snack later, or finding that you are the sort of person who doesn't particularly miss this meal. Hunger will only result if the child is refused any food two hours later. This is not a natural consequence, but a parentally decided-upon consequence meant to teach the child a lesson.

Jade has had a series of late nights. At the end of the week she has an important tennis match that she is competing in. By the time she arrives, Jade is feeling very negative about her match. She is late, stressed and ill-tempered and has had a row with the mother, who has told her for the thousandth time that she is making herself ill and will play badly. As predicted the match goes badly and Jade knows that the first thing her mother will say as she comes off the court is 'I told you so.' Jade knows by heart the lecture about how she can't play tennis and have late nights; a lecture that always ends, 'this is just the consequence of your own silly actions, Jade.'

Is it? Jade's friend Tara wins her match that day and plays well, but Tara has also had some late nights, a few of them sitting up watching movies or playing music with Jade. This is what the girls enjoy doing on long summer evenings and all the rows about consequences with Jade's Mum haven't convinced the 14 year old girls to change their ways. The difference isn't that Tara has a lot more stamina; it is simply that their parents have different views about helping their child to get what she wants. Tara's parents let her sleep late in the mornings. They speak to her gently when she is feeling tired. They offer advice, but don't tell her that she is ruining her life or try to force her to bed. Tara's parents aren't at war with her and Tara knows this, so she more often slips in an occasional early night to ensure she can be up early when she has a match. Tara, like Jade, likes to be up late, but she makes more reasonable decisions and when she stretches herself she knows that her parents will be there to support her with high energy drinks, quiet support, chances to sleep at other times and non-manipulative advice.

There are times when bad things happen despite our best efforts to prevent them, but parents can go a long way to minimize such times. We can give lots of information about nutrition and body clocks and individual patterns of eating and how to get access to food at lots of different times. We can discuss the safest ways of climbing and the best kind of trees to use and find out about other climbing opportunities to extend these skills. We can ensure that children can sleep when it suits them and do not have to be artificially and forcefully woken or forced to sleep.

The cry often comes back, 'But how will he ever learn about…?' The simple answer is that children will learn through information and discussion. Children don't have to experience artificial consequences dressed up as 'natural' in order to learn the laws of physics or how their bodies work or what people's attitudes to different sorts of behavior might be. Children are not going to learn how to think clearly, reasonably and creatively about problems and how to overcome them by being fed a diet of lies about what will happen to them if they try out certain things. If there is a good reason why a child should not do something, then the reason should be able to stand for itself and not need the back up of made-up 'consequences'. If the reason not to do something does not stand up to scrutiny, it should be revised, not propped up by compulsion in the garb of 'nature' or 'common sense'.

- Most natural consequences aren't natural at all, they are imposed or avoidable; reason is a much better way to convince our children of something
- Children don't have to suffer to learn, quite the reverse; distress is a poor learning medium, unlike information and discussion.
- In all lives bad things happen from time to time; children will have their share of real problems to work through without their beloved parents constructing extra hardships for them.

7
Out of Control

All too often when we think about children who are getting what they want the image that springs to mind is of a spoiled brat who cares little or nothing for anyone else and whose life, if not already out of control, is spinning dangerously near the precipice. I am suggesting that children should get what they want and I want to reassure you that this is not parenting for the insane, but the parenting of the future. It certainly isn't conventional parenting as we know it and it will challenge most of what you've ever heard about parenting, not least all those dire fears about what will happen if you don't establish that the parents are the bosses from the outset of your child's life. Fear is at the root of most parental control. Moral panics are easy to engineer and we all know that parenting is a one-way ticket; we can't go back and make good our mistakes, so we are understandably nervous. In this chapter I want to deconstruct that fear.

Many parents are afraid that if we are not the ones controlling the child's behavior, then that behavior will be 'out of control' rather than within the child's control. Much of this fear arises from witnessing situations where parental control has disintegrated or where parents are so disengaged from their children that the children make increasingly bizarre bids to be noticed. Parents might point to children who are both anti-social and self-destructive and say, 'Look, his parent didn't manage to control him, so we will have to try harder if we don't want our children to end up like that.' Others argue, 'Look, her parents took no interest and simply let her do anything she liked, no questions asked, and what a mess that's resulted in.' These are not arguments against living consensually within our families.

The prisons are not full of children from consent seeking homes and whilst this style of parenting is not primarily concerned with producing glossy child 'products,' I think we can confidently predict that this will remain the case. Self-destructive people who seem to be as much beyond their own powers of control as anyone else's are not reasonable, creative, undamaged individuals. Self-destructive people are damaged people, not those happily pursuing their own best interests.

On the Same Side as Children

Child control is a war game. Amongst its armory are 1001 techniques that aid and abet parental triumph, including some damaging myths, everything from 'If you don't eat cabbage you will suffer for life' to the darker side of fantasy, 'if you're not good, Father Christmas won't bring you any presents.' Living by consent entails being honest with our children, not using intimidation, however dressed up to be cute and cuddly.

We can't engage in parenting that is reasonable, based on sharing information and gives children the safety to change their minds if we are relying on lies as a means of control. What's more, such means of control are essentially limited and, although they might reap immediate compliance, they are also likely to reap eventual scorn and resistance. Trying to enforce control is stressful; you have to constantly oppose yourself to your offspring. It is also a short-term solution, sooner or later the lies lead to mistrust and an answering volley of deceitful subterfuge learnt from you, the parent.

Daisy wants a doll's house for Christmas, just like the one her friend Stephanie has. Daisy's mother has told her that she must keep her room tidy for six weeks before she will consider the request; after all, Father Christmas won't bring presents to little girls who are messy and who would only lose all the pieces. Five year old Daisy spends weeks failing to meet the required standards of tidiness. Somehow the whole process of tidying her room just overwhelms her and her feelings of failure and anxiety don't assist her to find better ideas about tidiness. On Christmas morning Daisy wakes not with excitement, but with trepidation. However, downstairs, there is the longed for doll's house after all. Daisy is thrilled, but also confused. Was her room tidy enough after all? No, her mother tells her, but Father Christmas is very kind and must have thought that she had been a 'good girl' in lots of other ways. Not only is Daisy still a failure, not only were her mother's predictions about Father Christmas wrong and untrustworthy, but now there is this amorphous standard of 'being good' that she has no idea how she is meeting or how she might fall from grace.

Of course, this is just the stuff of any normal childhood; getting them to behave or at least trying to do so with the aid of a fairy story never did a child any harm, did it? Well, it certainly is 'normal' and, since we can't see into the minds of others, it would be unhelpful to overstate the possible damage caused, but it would be just as unhelpful to trivialize it simply on the grounds that it is a common childhood experience. Sharing stories about Father Christmas is not the issue here and nor is joining in a joint fantasy to promote family fun, but using tradition as a control tool is simply force by another name. Daisy isn't helped to develop better tidying ideas and neither is her mother, so the problem at hand is unresolved. Worse still, Daisy has lost some confidence in herself and in her mother's truthfulness. Whether or not this was actually a big deal for Daisy, it is the case that things could have been more pleasant for everyone involved. Control techniques generally require two opposing sides, whereas living by consent requires that everyone is on the same side looking for mutual solutions.

Living by consent is sabotaged when parents repeatedly use myths, adages, so-called 'white' lies and half-baked misinformation to manipulate their children. It may seem innocuous to spout fables to convince a three year old to go to bed on Christmas Eve or to tell a five year old that he will be in mortal pain if he misses a tooth brushing session or to convince a ten year old that it is best if all her TV viewing is censored. It may even be that these instances of compulsion will in fact be the ones that do no particular harm, though we can never see inside another mind to know. However when children are subjected to a lifetime of such 'little' manipulations they might also build into ingrained and poor ideas. In addition these manipulations contribute to the eventual understanding in so many children that their parents, far from being trusted advisors to whom they can go for information, should not be listened to with anything but a large pinch of salt. It is hardly any wonder that so many children decide that their parents must not know too much about their lives.

When Tracey is considering unprotected sex at fifteen which parent is going to help her to be safe, moral and make the best decisions? The authoritarian controller who uses scare tactics and continually grounds her? The permissive negligent parent who tells her to do whatever she feels like doing? The loving liberal who wants to give some information, but can't help peppering it with communications which leave Tracey feeling that she is letting down the family? The consent seeking parent, who communicates her own moral stance, helps Tracey to find the best information and remains respectful?

- Child control is a war game that relies on an armory of techniques that you use against your child.
- Control is a short-term measure that damages trust and is liable to foster a wealth of subterfuge techniques in response.
- Using fables and white lies to manipulate children is simply another form of compulsion that adds to their confusion.
- Parents can be controllers whose opinions are to be doubted or neglect their children or become trusted advisers who will refrain from compulsion.

- Control does not make children safer. It diminishes their internal resources to problem solve creatively and it lessens the chance that they will consult parents on important issues for fear of compulsion.

The Age of Reason

Growing up is fraught with risk and no matter what sort of parent we choose to be we will sometimes get it wrong and so will our children. Guilt is a futile emotion, but learning and doing the best we possibly can is always a possibility. To maximize the possibility of doing the best, many child-rearing books promise that establishing control at a tender age is the parents' best chance of retaining it through the difficult teens and ending up with the 'right' kind of children. Consent-based parenting, on the other hand, is never about control. Moreover, you don't have to start at any particular age in order to reap the benefits.

For those who are fortunate enough to discover consent-based parenting before they have children or when their children are very young, there is no need to wait for some magical 'age of reason' before living in win-win ways. The needs of young babies may be intense, but, in general, they are fairly simple in range. Food, warmth and physical closeness tend to feature high on the list. Despite the lack of verbal articulacy, most parents quickly become adept at interpreting the signals of what is liked and disliked. This is what it means to credit babies with reasonableness; they are learning all the time and following their inner wishes and self-interest. The same is true as babies grow into toddlers. We may only be able to use very simple words or we may need to rely on visual or practical demonstration, but we can definitely discern toddlers' preferences, and clearly see that toddlers are able to move on to new preferences or (in their own way) suggest new solutions to adults. Reasonableness does not require that children first reach a golden age of reason. It simply relies on not interfering with children's ability to express preferences and not preventing them from reaching new and mutual preferences.

Let's take Hanif, a nine-month-old who comes across a bottle of bleach and starts trying to unscrew the lid. The neglectful solution is to leave him to it. He'll soon learn not to mess with bleach! The forceful strategy is to take the bleach away from Hanif, probably with a firm 'no', perhaps with an attempt at distraction if Hanif is in a more liberal household. The common-sense rationale is that the bleach could do Hanif harm and that compulsion is a lesser harm than the risks of swallowing bleach. For Hanif, something else is happening. His needs and desires are not being

taken seriously. He begins to learn that, whilst his parents say they love him, they will still do mean things to him (by his lights).
Already, Hanif is being given mixed messages about the correlation of love and hurt.

We need not glibly let our children fend for themselves, but we can work with the child to find something the child would prefer to play with or drink or shake or smell. It might be that Hanif simply wants a drink. It might be that Hanif would like a bottle of some harmless liquid that he can screw, unscrew, pour and smell. It might be that this particular bottle is attractive and feels good to hold. Could the bleach be emptied into another container, the bottle scoured and another liquid put in to retain the feel? It might be that Hanif would prefer an ice cream or a trip to the park or a big bowl of finger paint or corn flour mixture to anything that the bottle could offer. The point is that it is highly unlikely that nine-month-old Hanif was trying to commit suicide with the bleach. It is possible for an adult on his side to work with him to find what he wanted to get out of the exploration, and to enable him to achieve it or move on to another better exploration.

- No age is too young to begin respecting a child, but neither is it ever 'too late' to begin.
- Control is rarely something parents exert from any but the best intentions, but the fact remains that it allows children to confuse love and hurt, which in turn damages the child's ability to think reasonably.
- Having a parent who is on your side and is willing to find solutions that everyone prefers builds an environment that is both safe and preferable.

Freedom Now

Many people persist in thinking that whilst finding consent is a great ideal, surely we have to phase it in and give a little freedom at a time, until children reach adulthood and can be trusted? No, children are not works in process who become the finished product at the age of sixteen or eighteen; they are complete people here and now. Our parenting needs to reflect that. The notion that children can be given incremental freedom as they get older and become 'more reasonable' is a pervasive one. In particular, babies and toddlers are targeted as the main focus of rule-bound parenting, but there is also a widespread resistance to the idea that younger children as a group can live without compulsion. From sharp tools to fires to staying out alone, there are assumptions about externally imposed safety rules shared by conventional parenting and education. I want to argue that these actually compromise safety by stopping children from gaining experience of self-motivated decisions made in a safe and supportive environment.

Imagine two seven-year-old friends, Sadie and Paul. They have just made an outdoor den in a field at the back of Paul's house. They decide that they will have a feast in their new hide-away and Sadie runs home to collect some crisps and sweets. Paul returns without any food as his Mum has told him that she doesn't want him to spoil his appetite for tea. Disappointed, Paul suggests that they can pick some food of their own and turns his attention to some nearby berries. Sadie says they should ask an adult what they are. She says that she knows that some berries are delicious and good and others are harmful, even deadly. Paul replies that this is silly. He insists that berries are just fruit and adds that if he asks his Mum he will just be shouted at and maybe smacked, because he is not allowed to eat anything that his Mum considers dirty and he isn't supposed to eat between meals. Sadie tries again to convince Paul that they could ask Sadie's Mum, who has told her that some berries can hurt you even if you only take a little bit and that smaller bodies can get more hurt. She says that her Mum has told her that some berries aren't so strong and might just give you tummy ache or not do anything bad if you tried a bit. She points out that she and Paul don't know what sort these are, so they really should ask someone to help them. Paul,however, insists that a bit won't hurt and he's not risking asking an adult.

Paul's information is much sketchier than Sadie's, because his rule-bound parents have replaced information with the simplistic rule of 'don't touch.' Paul sees his parents as the opposition, to be thwarted, and hopes to be able to get away with doing something without their knowledge. Sadie knows that her parents would help her to make her own good decision and would not treat her as though she was an irrational or suicidal idiot. Paul knows no such thing and the chance of being able to indulge in a forbidden activity over-rides his reasonableness and his friend's protests. Having a child who will seek advice before making informed decisions is a much safer option.

Even if we succeed in making our children live by rules, even if we can make them accept rules without having to resort to physical punishment, even if we choose our rules carefully and only impose a few rules that will tend to hold in most cases; even then, our children will not be as safe as children who are given honest information about risks; children who know that they can get all the help they need in negotiating risks, and are accustomed to finding the best solution for any particular situation.

We can't foresee every situation. Life is risky, and there will always be tragedies whatever way we parent. The children most likely to be safe are those who can think most reasonably, who can access advice without fear of compulsion or lies, and who have no motivation to do something just because it is forbidden. Children who are brought up to find win-win solutions will certainly take risks, but they will take them reasonably, advisedly, and with the best preparation, to get the learning they want without exposure to unnecessary and unwanted danger. Ultimately, the only safety that any individual has is that which comes from her inner motivation. Assisting our children in developing this safety does them an enormous service. Forcing them to accept safety rules that they are not internally convinced of only leaves them exposed and vulnerable to irrational decisions.

Remember Tim from chapter two who began life as a toddler who wanted to touch the fire? Tim's life could be so much more satisfying in a consent seeking household where risks and experiments can be assessed with trusted advice and where Tim could develop good assumptions about fire, pursue his own learning and stay safe. Sometimes we choose risks quite reasonably in order to learn something or enjoy some particular experience, but many other dangers are avoidable. The safest course is to parent our children so that they will trust our advice, critically assess our best ideas and make their own rational decisions.

- Children do not become gradually more human and should not be treated as such.
- Children's lack of experience and information is not an indication that they need rules, but that they require engaged parents who will act as trusted advisors.
- No form of parenting can make life risk free, but children are most safe when they can critically assess advice and do not suspect that they are not being manipulated.

Children Are Not 'Asking For It'

Children want to know that their parents really care. Having parents who simply can't be bothered with all the inconvenient and enormously time consuming activities of being engaged parents is demeaning. On the other hand, most parents, whilst they don't relish conflict, believe that some compulsion and conflict are all part and parcel of being a parent. This idea is strengthened when adults look back on their childhoods and wish that their own parents had been more forceful, not less. Many of us have those thoughts; if only my mother had made me practice the piano; if only I'd been forced to stay away from those bad influences. This combination of parental responsibility and wistful regret seem to make certain acts of compulsion not only more credible, but even more loving. We need to think again; I want to suggest that children, no matter how self destructively they might seem to be behaving, are not simply begging for their parents to come in and make them do the right thing.

Children certainly want parental involvement; they do not want to feel abandoned, but it is not necessary for that involvement to be forceful or manipulative. Consensual family relationships require a very high level of parental engagement, but still hold out a model of win-win solutions. So what of all those desires that we as adults have looking back on parents who didn't make us do certain things? Are we really longing for retrospective compulsion or would we have been happier simply to have had more parental engagement? In so many cases when we look back to missed opportunities we are looking back on situations of conflict. It is understandable that it didn't produce what we now think we wanted from life, but that is no indication that more compulsion would have served us any better. Would I really be the great piano player I dream about if I'd been compelled to practice or would I be someone who hates piano music, associating it with pain and conflict? We can't know. Simply because we wish for some skill now does not prove that it could have been foisted on us at an earlier age without causing damage.

Children who are in distress are not begging for boundaries or just asking for their parents to step in and take control, but they may be desperately in need of information, input and family structures that foster their self-reliance without abandoning them to their own devices. Boundaries and control are often used to make the lives of children safe and to communicate parental care and involvement. The motives for this are good, but the result can be a gradual undermining of the child's self-worth and their trust in parents as engaged, but non-manipulative advisors. Children whose inner motivation, resourcefulness and reasonableness are respected can develop a sense of safety and being cared for that goes far beyond what any artificial boundary or parental compulsion can ever achieve. Children whose lives are focused on finding the best and most creative ways to meet their preferences now and who operate on the assumption that present problems have solutions are very unlikely to be those who grow up and wistfully look back longing for parental compulsion.

Carmen is the youngest child with four older brothers. Her parents are liberal and go a long way towards finding consent in the family. The family started out practicing attachment-style parenting, long-term breastfeeding, and the children have a lot of control over their own lives.

Carmen has some severe medical problems and these put enormous restrictions on her diet. From time to time, particularly when Carmen is with friends who do not have such restrictions, she longs to eat foods that will make her ill. Her parents will remind her of the problems and, if all else fails, they use compulsion. It is very much a last resort in their eyes, but one that they think is preferable to the pain and distress Carmen will feel the next day after eating the 'wrong' food. Even more occasionally, Carmen finds herself in a situation where she is able to eat a 'wrong' food without her parents being able to prevent her. The result is that she is ill the next day, in some pain and generally very upset. Carmen's parents, although they hate resorting to compulsion, are very clear that Carmen is clearly unable to think about food reasonably and feel that these incidents highlight Carmen's need to have them control her food intake and to set safe boundaries for her.

The situation is a vicious, self-fulfilling circle despite Carmen's parents' best intentions. Carmen knows that the bottom line is that she will be compelled and that negotiation and democracy is limited; autonomy over her own body is never going to be hers. Her parents, desperately concerned for their daughter's well being, persist in adding compulsion into the situation, making Carmen less and less able to think reasonably about food and then citing her irrationality to 'prove' to her that she needed the compulsion in the first place.

What might happen if Carmen's parents began to act as trusted advisers instead of final arbiters and stopped seeing her as irrational and self-destructive? Perhaps Carmen might immediately eat something that would make her ill. This doesn't prove that she should have her freedom removed, but merely indicates that she needs her parents to be very supportive and helpful whilst she finds better solutions that take account of who she really is; a person who happens to have a medical problem amongst many other things. If Carmen does not see her parents immediately rushing to remove her new found liberty then she may well become much more open to listening to their ideas about food. They, in their turn, might begin to consider that there are times when it is reasonable for Carmen to wander from her diet in some way in order to explore something that is more important at the time to her learning and growth as an individual. This may mean finding clever substitutes or it may mean finding better medical ways of supporting the occasional ill effects or it may simply mean giving her a lot of love and support to cope with physical pain. It is possible that Carmen may quite reasonably consider occasional physical pain is much less damaging than being treated as an example of a medical problem group instead of as a unique individual. She may think the pain of compulsion with all the damage it does to how she is able to think about food and health and fun is much worse than the occasional physical ill effects of a wrong food. If her parents can appreciate this and stop using compulsion to 'help' their daughter then Carmen will be able to consider their input for what it is; the advice and best ideas of people who care passionately and who she can trust not to compel her if she disagrees.

- Caring and coercing should not be confused.
- Distress is not a cry for compulsion and boundaries, but a sign that there is already damaging compulsion at work in the situation.

8
Private: Keep Out

The line between trusted advisor and intrusive saboteur can be a fine one. In the realm of personal decisions, there is often a huge amount of tension between parents and children, whether the pierced teenager or the two year old who knows exactly which flimsy party dress she wants to wear to play in the rain. A huge amount of this tension simply melts away when we convince ourselves that children are agents of their own lives and a large amount of what goes on in their personal realm is none of our business. That is not the same as saying we cease to care. If we think our best friend will not get the job in a high powered legal chambers if she goes ahead with her plan to have all over body tattoos we would be a poor friend not to say so, but we would also normally expect to offer our opinions without force. Of course we care for our children more than even our closest friends, but care can be expressed without compulsion; care is not an excuse to invade someone's personal domain.

Valuing someone's personal space highly, even when the other person is your child, does not mean that you need to run your household on the basis of rights. Human rights are very important when it comes to how large numbers of people interact, but usually in a household we don't need to stand on our rights. Thomas may have no 'right' to comment that his son's room smells so badly that he finds it difficult to pass by, but they share a home and Thomas has a responsibility to help his son find new ideas for living with people. A father and son should be able to put aside the impersonal mechanism of 'rights' in favor of finding mutual solutions. When the trusted advisor role is working well and our children really trust that our opinions are not the beginning of compulsion, it is likely that parents will be given far more access to their children's lives than conventional parents would. After all, saying 'no' on principal and holding on to parental authority and threatening punishment have a proven track record of children resorting to lying or secretly engaging in dangerous behavior without any advice.

- Children, like other human beings have a personal realm that it is not our right to invade.
- Living by consent involves close personal relationships and a bare acknowledgement of rights is only ever a poor default.
- Instead we should aim at finding mutual solutions without compromising each other's personal freedom.

- When compulsion is removed from the relationship, children are much more likely to be motivated to find mutual solutions with us, even in areas that impinge on their personal space.

Children Are People Too

Children have a lot more to them than can ever be known by anyone, even those closest to them. Knowing our children gives us clues as to what they want and how we can best help them in life, but their 'unknowability' also has to be kept in mind.

We all, adults and children alike, have areas in which our thinking is poor, where we act irrationally or our ideas are ingrained. Knowing that children, like us, have their flaws can sometimes tempt parents to discount certain of their children's ideas; it is easy to decide that a child is only saying she wants ice cream for breakfast because she's irrational. This is a dangerous trap. No-one can see into another's mind. While children aren't perfect it is not helpful to guess which bits of them are faulty especially since compulsion may only make them more irrational.

The tendency to set our ideas about our own children in stone is one of the easiest parenting errors to fall into. A distant aunt might expect that we will be able to rattle off a list of our children's defining characteristics in order to fix them in their mind: Jeanette is a tomboy, Alan is rather hyperactive, Joe has reading difficulties. The trouble with these seemingly innocuous remarks is that they act a bit like a photograph; they freeze one moment and blow it up into a definition of who the child is and ever shall be. They fix the child according to outside observations.

On one hand, it seems obvious that we are more likely to be able to help our children get what they want from life if we have handy thumb-nail pictures of them. The trick is not to treat someone as a packaged personality type, but to remember that every child is a unique, constantly changing individual. We constantly make observations about one another and these are fine as long as we do not fall into the trap of having a fixed idea about what Jeanette will do or want on every future occasion. We should not, for example, start channeling Jeanette down pre-set routes that fit in with our perceptions and observations. Rather, we should be tentative about the suggestions we make based on our observations. No matter how much time we spend together, we never know what is going on inside someone else's head so observations should never become fixed ideas.

Consider Jason, an eleven-year-old who doesn't exhibit fluent literacy to the observing world. His parents observe that

Jason has a lot of energy and appears (to them) to be often frustrated and destructive. Instead of rushing to have Jason diagnosed with ADHD, medicated with Ritalin, labeled as having a specific learning difficulty and plugged into a remedial reading program, Jason's parents try a different approach. They make suggestions about how they think he is frustrated, they work with him to find out what he wants to get out of reading and work with him to achieve what he wants in ways that don't presume to 'fix' Jason or derail his internal learning processes.

Instead of listing observations to fix our children we can:

- Acknowledge that our observations are tentative and subjective.
- Be open to changing our minds.
- Concentrate on solving the present problem and finding out what the child wants rather than trying to guess what's in his mind; 'I might be wrong, but I got the idea you wanted to read that book and had a bit of difficulty. Can I help?' 'You don't seem to like being woken up in the mornings, can we find a better way of starting the day?'

Not What Parents Expect

When we hold our perfect newborn in our arms it's so tempting to imagine and plan life for them. Then reality intervenes; we realize that our children are not living the life we dreamed. Far from filling us with horror, this is actually a good thing. Children don't have to do what we expect in order to thrive. In fact children can find many routes to getting what they want from life that may look odd to us, but aren't as irrational as first glance suggests.

A relatively young child, Billy, decides that a local Sunday School is a good place to hear stories and meet other children. All goes well until the teacher begins to expound ideas about creationism. Billy objects with some scientific ideas he has learnt from home and is informed that it is wicked not to accept creationism. He is left with the definite impression that he must accept the doctrine or lose the teacher's approval. Billy, however, comes from a home where compulsion is not normal. He is used to the idea that people disagree and will choose a theory on its own merits and with a reasonable appraisal, knowing that he does not risk parental disapproval and that neither is his well being dependent on his teacher's approval. Children who are not weighed down with other people's expectations, but who are simply given access to lots of information are much less malleable, even when they are in inflexible environments.

The pressure of expectations, on the other hand, can be damaging not only in its most overt forms, but also when it is employed with subtlety. A parent may not directly express disappointment in a child's decision, but there are many ways of expressing disappointment through looks, sighs or negative asides that can put the child into a state of distress and conflict.

I once had a conversation with a mother who believed that certain TV programs 'compelled' her children to hold distasteful opinions. She allowed them to watch TV, but noted with satisfaction that her children only 'chose' 'bad' programs when she was out, so as not to offend her by watching 'rubbish.' It seems to me that that information is being communicated in a way that is laden with expectations. The mother not only shares her ideas, but does so repeatedly with no sense that she could be wrong. Moreover, although she overtly tells her children that they 'may' watch what they please she uses subtle communication to make them have to choose between their own ideas and her approval.

Of course parents have ideas and a wealth of experience and information that it is only right that they should fully share with their children. However, if we want to avoid compulsion, these ideas need communicating without the overlay of expectations. Parental approval should not be conditional on adopting certain ideas. Information shared fully and frankly is a vital part of parent-child interaction. Expectation, on the other hand, introduces a desire to manipulate someone else's mind.

- Provided children have information and can make their own decisions, then coming into contact with inflexible environments or poor ideas need not be a problem.
- Parents should share lots of information and their best ideas with children, but should stop short of adding their expectations, whether overt or subtle.

But What If?

You think of your son as a unique individual who you want to help. You've given him your best ideas about life, the universe and personal hygiene, without any manipulation. Still, something in you cries out, 'But what if my five-year-old takes to a diet of coke and chocolate, pees on all my plants because he can't be bothered to walk to the bathroom, and insists on playing in the street at two in the morning?' Ask yourself, why do we assume that children might enter into self-destructive meltdown unless they are compelled not to? I believe it is simply because we have a very powerful meme that children are not reasonable. Sadly, it's easy to make this meme into a self-fulfilling vicious cycle by compelling children until they exhibit irrational behavior, then claiming we have to use force because they are unreasonable.

Children are not infallible, but children who are used to being respected and treated as full human beings have no reason to be wildly self-destructive, anti-rational or anti-social. Why should a child who believes that her parents are on her side, who knows that following her own interests will be supported and who trusts that solutions can be found, need to become a sociopath?

The argument that what we need is more control is false and is based on observing children who have been let down in various ways by conventional parenting. We cannot possibly be there controlling everything our child does from birth to sixteen years old. We physically cannot live their lives. Our children are going to be making decisions and they are going to be making some of those decisions alone. Having built up a repertoire of conversations about every aspect of morality, spent considerable time sharing ideas with our children and helping them remain and become creative, resourceful, reasonable problem solvers; we can expect that our children will make the best decisions by their own lights at that particular time. We should also expect that mistakes will be made, but making mistakes is an opportunity for learning, not a signal that our human dignity ought to be taken from us. Sometimes our children will not make the decisions that we would have made or advised. Raising independent individuals is not an exercise in getting our children to do exactly what we would want by roundabout, manipulative means, even in our absence.

- Children, like adults, are limited, but they are still individuals in the best position to make decisions about themselves, given proper parental support and input.
- "What if...?" is the wrong question. The real question is why would a child, who has been fully engaged with and treated as reasonable suddenly engage in anti-social destructive behavior?

'What if...?' may be the wrong question, but it's still the most frequently asked, so in the next sections I'll explore some of the most frequent 'what ifs' in more depth. First I'll address the general worry that children who are helped to get what they want will be spoiled brats, before moving on to more specific areas; if children are helped to get what they want aren't they going to want to eat nothing but junk, dress inappropriately, never help around the house, get into terrible trouble, perhaps even become promiscuous or addicted to drugs and generally have no sense of emergency or consequences? This isn't the case and the next sections will discuss why not.

A charter for brats

It can't be stressed too forcefully - the meme that 'giving children their own way will lead to selfish brats' is wrong. Even if we accept that extremes of anti-social behavior arise from extreme compulsion, either through abuse or neglect, we might still have reservations. Our children may not be likely to turn into mass murderers, but will they be pleasant people? Are they not more likely to be spoilt brats who grow into selfish adults?

Such questions arise from a number of misunderstandings. Why do we oppose self-interest and altruism? We are too used to the idea that if we are enjoying something, it must be at someone else's expense, whereas, if we are suffering, we are helping someone else. Is this really the case? As a parent, I can derive huge satisfaction and pleasure from helping my child get what he wants. It is something I prefer to do. I am at once pursuing my own and my child's interest. As a worker, I can derive enormous satisfaction from my job, or I can choose to do it to support the people I love or to benefit the community. These goals do not need to be mutually exclusive. I am doing what I prefer on one or many levels and others benefit. It is when we are following our passions that we are not only at our most self-interested and most creative, but also most likely to benefit others in a variety of ways.

Moreover, why should a child who wants what he wants be a 'brat'? What is it that makes us resent his clarity, self-knowledge and sense of self-worth? Are we threatened by attitudes that we were not allowed to develop ourselves as children? Are we afraid that it will mean that our own needs must be trampled? Do we worry that we will have to immediately jump to order and sacrifice ourselves to grasping children? If we have allowed ourselves to enter a cycle of self-surrendering martyrdom, then we need to address that problem rather than blame our children. Having children who can clearly state their preferences is a bonus in the process of finding mutual solutions, not a threat to our own sense of self or a sign that they are intransigent demanding monsters.

When children experience relationships of consent in which the needs of others can be taken seriously without infringing their own needs and wants, then they have no reason to fear the needs of others. When children experience the benefits of finding mutual solutions, then the needs and wants of others become part of the pool of resources available to them, rather than threats. A child who will not listen to anything other than his first preference and who irrationally clings to this when there may be solutions he could enjoy much more, is a child who is used to losing and is determined to resist losing again. Being 'self-centered' or 'pleasing ourselves' does not have to stand in opposition to finding mutual solutions and benefiting others. This is a false and pernicious dichotomy that living by consent can overcome.

When children are persistent about a particular preference it is easy for adults to assume that the child is being unreasonable or stubborn. What she might be doing, however, is offering challenges to our intransigently held assumptions. It is not beyond the realm of possibility that in this instance, we need to change.

Eleri is almost four and loves to draw for hours and hates being interrupted. She lives with her single parent Mum, Becca, in a rural area. Becca has little adult support and is responsible herself for all of the chores. Eleri doesn't enjoy being in the car, so Becca limits shopping trips to the town twenty miles away to one afternoon each week. Becca has bought a tray for Eleri's car seat so that Eleri can drawing, but still Eleri objects to every car trip. Eleri complains about the car seat straps, that the tray on the seat moves too much and that she can't move well enough to draw properly. Becca dreads shopping trips and hates to see Eleri distressed, but she reasons that safety must come first and it is illegal for Eleri to travel in the car without proper restraint. Becca also feels hurt by her daughter's constant tantrums. She is weary of the stress and of Eleri's ingratitude at all Becca's attempts to minimize the outings and make them as pleasant as possible. Becca feels as though nothing she does can ever be good enough and starts to wonder if Eleri is becoming a spoiled brat in response to all of Becca's careful consideration.

Becca sees Eleri as intransigent. Eleri sees her mother as intransigent (or might if she could it express it in those terms). Becca knows that Eleri hates the car seat, but still insists on putting her into it and then says horrible things when she objects, like, "I could slit my arm and bleed to death for you, and it still wouldn't be enough, would it?" Of course it wouldn't be enough! Parenting isn't about getting to a point where we've done 'enough;' it is an ongoing process. No matter how hard done by Becca is feeling it is highly unlikely that Eleri's distress is aimed at making Becca suffer. Eleri simply wants a solution.

Becca has to shop. Becca is committed to Eleri traveling safely. Eleri wants to draw in comfort. Both are stuck and in conflict. Becca doesn't have a lot of support in her life. Could she change this? She might decide to investigate Internet shopping, though the supermarket may tell her that they don't deliver to rural areas. Maybe she could befriend the elderly lady down the road who has the dog that Eleri loves to stroke. It might be possible that the lady would take care of Eleri on the shopping afternoons in exchange for Becca picking up shopping for her neighbor. Alternatively, Becca might do more research about car harnesses for children and discover a little padded table into which the middle lap belt fits with the belt and table holding the child securely. This would leave Eleri's upper arms free to draw in much more comfort as well as providing a better surface for her paper.

Even if the solution is difficult to come by, Becca should not assume that Eleri is simply stubborn and ungrateful. It might help if Becca stops using the word 'problem' and thinks about 'puzzles' instead. When we think of problems we often tend to revert to feeling we are the victim on some level, whereas puzzles merely demand new ideas. Most things that we feel stuck over owe more to lack of information than to any lack of real solutions. We have to let go of thinking that there is nothing we can do.

- Self-interest and altruism are not opposites and when we stop treating them as such a lot of creativity is released.
- The more children experience the benefits of finding mutual solutions, the less worried they will be about being open minded and considering the needs of others.
- Win-win outcomes breed more win-win outcomes.
- Adults, as well as children, need to start with open minds about the outcome. If you know how a situation must end then a solution is sabotaged before the discussion begins.
- Children who are used to a cycle of consent seeking have no need to express preferences simply as a way of hurting their parents; your suffering is not part of the solution and there is no need to imagine that your child wants it.
- There is always something we can do.

Eating junk?

Food is a common battleground between parents and children and an area where parents generally think we know best, but in this fast moving arena, where information and fads become confused, a little humility goes a long way. It is not simple to categorize food as 'good' or 'bad.' Foods that are 'good' for us in one decade are highly likely to be the very ones we are warned to avoid a few years later, yet this is an area of high parental anxiety.

If we stop trying to force our ideas about food onto children, what do we imagine might happen? Many parents believe that without restraint children would resort to a diet of chocolate and coke and never look at another vegetable again. Why? Do adults who have no one to monitor and regulate their food intakes routinely resort to irrational diets that might even endanger their health? Certainly, some do. However the likelihood is that adults with poor food ideas about food, who struggle all their lives with their relationship to food did not have childhoods where they could freely choose the foods they liked without 'good' or 'bad' labels being placed on them. It is much more likely that those of us with a thousand and one food hang-ups were told to eat up everything on our heaped up plates before being allowed pudding or suffered compulsion in one of a million ways that damaged our ability to think clearly about food. Compulsion has an appalling track record in relation to food, not just at the extremes of eating disorders, but right across the spectrum of yo-yo diets, poor self-image and ordinary enjoyment.

Surely, though, we can't simply let out children eat anything? As in other areas, we should share our ideas with our children as trusted advisors, but, tentatively and without scare mongering or overstatement. Leaving a solid object for several days in a glass of coke until it dissolves and then claiming that this is what will happen to your child's teeth if he drinks a glass of cola is, for example, extremely disingenuous. Cola is not the only acidic food and, in any case, drinking a glass of it is not the same as leaving your teeth to soak in it for days. Similarly, being able to demonstrate that a rat that eats a hundred weight of artificial sweeteners will develop cancerous tumors does not logically imply that one bag of gooey colored sweets will lead to death.

When we talk about food theories we need to be honest that these ideas are amongst some of the most highly contentious and fast changing that anyone holds. We also need to recognize that food is much more than merely functional. Simply determining what might be the best fuel input to keep bodies performing to peak specification is difficult and elusive, but even if we could prescribe the perfect diet for ensuring that we function as though we were cars in perfect factory conditions, it would still not be right to enforce this diet. We eat food for many reasons; including for pleasure, to experiment with new experiences or to give and receive hospitality. Food is not only about the elusive goal of physical perfection; we associate food with memories, emotions, places, seasons and more. When we experience compulsion around food our relationship with it inevitably deteriorates and our approach to eating is likely to become less rational.

Health is an important factor to take into consideration when we are choosing foods, and we do well as parents to share health related information about food in non-manipulative ways, but health is not the only consideration. Enjoyment and preference are also important considerations and, ultimately, a child's self image and self determination is more important even than perfect dental health. Children may well drink some cola, eat sweets when they feel like it or want to visit fast food restaurants occasionally. The same children may also choose to be vegetarians or vegans or love fish soup or broccoli or olives. Some children may actually not even like cola, chips or ice cream. Developing a good relationship with food is complex and judging another person's diet as 'bad' is unlikely to take account of all the factors in the other person's mind.

So how do we deal with situations where certain foods set off particular reactions in children? Firstly, we need to be aware that there is a whole industry of compulsion around preventing children from eating things they like under the guise that they make them ill or hyperactive, so we should proceed with caution.

Zach comes from a vegan home and his mother has told him that milk chocolate contains crushed up cows' bones that will make him sick. On a few occasions when someone has brought chocolate into his house, Zach has eaten some he has thrown up violently. Each time his mother has told him all about how horrible the chocolate really is and has warned him how ill he would be and each time she has been proved right. However, one day at a friend's house Zach is offered some chocolate. No-one mentions crushed cows' bones or how ill he will be and everyone else is enjoying the chocolate. Zach eats it and experiences no ill effects.

Dawn is in a similar situation in regard to fizzy drinks and squash. Her parents are convinced that the additives make Dawn hyperactive and that she should avoid them at all costs. Although Dawn's parents notice that she becomes what they term 'hyperactive' at other times when she has not eaten or drunk anything with additives, they still persist with the belief that it is the additives that are responsible for her behavior. If Dawn manages to have a glass of fizzy orange at a birthday party she is quite likely to oblige her parents with the expected behavior, bolstering their belief. However, they never stop to consider how their constant re-enforcing of their ideas about additives might be influencing Dawn. They certainly never consider that all the subtle signals they give off when Dawn drinks squash might play a major role to play in how Dawn acts out their assumptions.

In many cases it is almost impossible to conclude categorically that chocolate or fizzy drinks cause certain behaviors. Drawing such a conclusion is even more dubious when there is parental compulsion or subtle communication about expected bad effects. Sometimes, we do know that there are real effects. A child who is diabetic, for instance, faces real and possibly dangerous outcomes if she does not take her dietary needs seriously. Even in this situation, however, there is an opportunity to reach solutions that are best for her individual circumstances. Children who are accustomed to being respected don't want to kill themselves; they simply want solutions.

If we let go of our own irrational fears about foods and find solutions to real problems, there still might remain concerns about foods that make us uncomfortable. Willow is a vegan. She believes that doing no harm should be an attitude that extends to all life forms, and that she has no right to take other lives to feed herself. She is appalled by intensive farming techniques. Willow wants to raise her daughter, India, by finding consent, but she is very eager to pass on her vegan ideals. India goes along with the vegan diet until the age of ten, but by then she is increasingly aware that there are competing food theories and that several people she respects do not share her mother's views of animals. After some research, India decides that she would like to extend her diet. However, Willow objects that she should not be forced into preparing foods that offend her moral values.

Firstly, we have to be very wary of accusing children of forcing or compelling adults to do anything. Willow is the adult and it is she who holds the power. It can be very manipulative and undermining to make a child think that she is bullying her mother simply because she wants a new solution to the foods they eat. India has no power to enforce her preference and is in no position to compel Willow. Secondly, Willow is clearly putting her own ideas above her daughter's independence. She has forgotten that she may be wrong. She has forgotten that even if she is right the only moral way to convince another free person is with reason, not force. Thirdly, there are always solutions if we pursue them long and hard enough. If Willow finds certain things difficult to cook she might arrange for a friend to help India learn some basic cooking skills or look at ways of buying and preparing non vegan foods that involve very little effort on her part. Ready cooked meat, prepared meals, bought pies, soups etc are all available without Willow having to engage in the processes of preparing non vegan ingredients. Our moral views are very important, sometimes they are also right, but either our reasons stand up to another's scrutiny or they do not. Being right does not give us an excuse to behave badly towards a child for whom we are responsible.

If we do cease to control our children's diets, another anxiety is about the affect on the family budget. Reasonable children don't expect us to bankrupt the family providing meals; each family will find their own solutions within their own budget.

Another problem that parents often raise is that food choice will entail parents becoming constant cooks serving up several meals at each mealtime. This can be much less daunting than it sounds. Cooking aids like microwaves and toasters can make food preparation much simpler, as can keep a range of meals prepared and frozen on stand by. Many children enjoy being able to do things for themselves and as they get older can contribute to preparing meals or parts of meals. Most families will also find that there are a few staples that everyone enjoys eating together. Between all of these options, preparing spaghetti Bolognese for two children whilst another has a baked potato with cheese and beans, another has a burger and Mum and Dad have a lamb stew (previously cooked and frozen in portions) can take as little time as preparing one main meal. Moreover, it is much less likely to result in waste, tension and confrontation.

- Compelling children in relation to food is a high-risk strategy; likely to result in a lifetime of poor food theories.
- Children are not machines who should be maintained according to factory specifications by adding the perfect fuel (the so called 'good' foods). Food is not simply functional; health and dental care are factors to consider, but there are also many other complex and personal factors involved in diet that are about unique individuals.
- We need to be very wary of attributing behavioral effects to foods; it is impossible to single out other factors like expectations or compulsion. It is not only poor science, but also a poor way of relating to someone we care for.
- When food is part of a real problem situation (e.g. diabetes) then the answer is not compulsion, but reasonable and creative engagement to find solutions.
- Our own ideas about specific foods are not more important that our children's happiness, even if we happen to be right. Being right is not an excuse to behave immorally.
- Practical issues like family budget, time spent cooking or preparing foods we find difficult to handle ourselves are simply puzzles to be solved.

What do you look like?

How much energy and angst have you wasted on your child's wardrobe? Was it worth it? Diet, exercise, personal hygiene, health, sleep and clothing are all areas that present themselves as areas where control is needed. Adults constantly revise and develop ideas in these areas, yet we expect our children to develop good ideas whilst being compelled. There are three issues to consider. First, do we have any right to pass judgment on personal matters? Second, assuming we should share our ideas, are they correct? Third, even if we have the right to comment and our opinions are correct, is this a sufficient reason to hinder someone else's personal freedom?

Firstly, do we have the right to pass comment on what are essentially very personal matters? If we were asked that question in relation to another adult, the likely answer would be 'no'. We recognize that people have the right to eat what they like, bathe when they like, keep fit in their own way (or not), sleep when it suits them and choose their own clothes. However, even if we are able to see that children deserve the same rights to a personal domain as adults, we might object that when we are living in close proximity with others, we don't expect them to assert their rights all the time. We might, for example, feel that it is not unreasonable to expect a certain level of personal hygiene from a husband or wife, or we might reasonably request a partner to wear a particular style of clothing for an important company dinner party. In the same way, we share space with our children. Although we have no right as such to dictate what they eat, when they shower, whether they should use deodorant and how much sleep they need, it can be quite reasonable to share our assumptions about these areas and to seek mutual solutions. This does not mean that children should automatically accept our assumptions. It is simply a recognition that in close relationships there is an arena for comment and sharing, provided it does not become manipulative and provided that the parent is willing to desist if no mutual solution is found.

Mandy is a teenager who is experimenting with her looks and dress. Some of her choices seem rather daring to her parents, but they are keen to respect her choices. Mandy is also interested in religious beliefs and practices. She tells her parents that she wants to spend some time visiting different places of worship, finding out more about different beliefs and what they might mean for her. Her parents advise her that her favorite short red skirt is likely to be seen negatively at both the local Church and the Mosque a few streets away. They tell her that she may not be taken seriously, and may even meet with hostility. They suggest that more conventional clothing might help if she wants to be able to talk to people without eliciting negative judgments. Mandy decides that this is good advice and follows it.

A few weeks later her father tells her that some distant relatives are coming to stay. He says that they are rather conventional people who expect to be deferred to by young people. He asks that Mandy wear 'sensible' clothes while they are staying. Mandy thinks about this and decides that it is a bad idea. She tells her father that, in her own home, she feels that it is an unacceptable intrusion to dress according to the prejudices of virtual strangers whom she may very well never see again. She lets her father know that, while she was willing to make changes in order to visit other people in their own place of worship and to enable her to learn the most from her visits, she cannot see that this is a similar situation. She sympathizes with the fact that her father will probably get adverse comments from these relatives, but she thinks that he is quite able to deal with this in his own home with people with whom he has no regular contact. After some thought, her father agrees that Mandy is right. He can probably deflect any criticism with gentle humor and need not be so anxious about the visit.

While we do not have a right to tell our children what to eat or wear, it is reasonable for us to make suggestions and share opinions, though we always need to remember that our assumptions might be wrong.

To sleep perchance...

When it comes to issues of bodily autonomy, food (which we have already discussed above) and sleep are the two areas that seem to recurrently cause the most concern, yet they are also areas where compulsion can cause harm, as the number of adults with diet and sleep problems amply bears out.

Of course children need to sleep and some general information about sleep can be useful. We know, for example that younger children tend to need larger amounts of sleep and that the change in hormone levels generally means that teenage boys don't need to sleep until late evening, but still often need around ten hours sleep. These things can provide useful information, but they don't replace anyone's individual needs or take into account the fine details of individual body clocks and preferences.

Sometimes this will mean that there are problems to be solved. How does the mother of a baby who seems to be a night owl function well when she has two other children who are wide awake in the day? How does the teenage boy get up early for school or his Saturday job when his body wants to go to sleep late at night and get up late in the morning? How do parents get some private, quiet time in a house where none of the children have a set bedtime to adhere to? The solutions are as various as the families and resourcefulness involved; there is not one blueprint, but what will be the case for anyone seeking to live by consent is that the solutions will not involve deciding ahead what the outcome must be or seeking to impose any pre-ordained agenda.

Do you remember Alex? Alex is our lively four-year-old who has an older sister, Jenny, who is seven, and a baby brother, Jack. His Mum, Emma, is becoming increasingly exhausted and she is feeling very alone with her problems since her partner, Steve, works long hours and is away from home several nights each week. Emma is breastfeeding and this means being available at night.

Baby Jack and Jenny both sleep by eight and Emma would like to sleep then too, at least on the evenings when Steve is not home, so that she can catch up. Alex is seen as the problem in all of this. Alex needs very little sleep and eight o'clock is too early for him.

Firstly Emma needs to take a deep breath and remind herself that Alex isn't deliberately choosing a sleep pattern on the basis of being as annoying as possible to his mother. Alex has always been like this and, in the full knowledge of this, Emma and Steve decided to have a third child. It isn't reasonable for Emma to feel resentment towards Alex or to accuse him of being an awkward little monster who is driving her mad. Be that as it may, Emma needs to solve the problem now and the best way is with reason and resourcefulness, not compulsion.

Finding what will work varies with every family, but possible solutions might include building more exercise into Alex's day, finding activities that will occupy Alex safely and happily for a couple of evenings each week in a room next to Emma so that she can sleep even though he is awake, organizing some sleepover swaps with the mothers of Alex's friends so that some evenings each week will be quieter, as well as adding a fun activity into Alex's life (if he likes the idea), buying in some help, talking to Steve about temporary or permanent changes in his work patterns, finding a playgroup that Alex enjoys and taking a nap in the daytime with baby Jack. None of these solutions might be the particular one that works, but as long as Emma is determined that there is a possible solution and keeps working on it, then the likelihood of her finding a consensual solution is very high.

- Families live together in close proximity and mutual solutions that have the genuine consent of everyone are much more suited to family life than standing on our rights.
- Our special relationship with our children means that we can and should share ideas (as far as children are willing to hear them) even about issues which might normally be personal, but this should always stop short of compulsion and we should desist when asked.
- Living together means we affect each other's lives, so issues such as sleep may require searching for mutual solutions.

Chores for all

When the ordinary work of household chores has turned into the practice arena for war of the worlds, we need to start examining some new ideas. Many conflicts seem to reach an impasse simply because we oppose the supposed 'good of the family' group against the preferences of the individuals in the family. In fact, if one of its members is in distress, the good of the family group will never be served either; the group's good only becomes a possibility when everyone within it prefers what is happening. It is a truism of conventional parenting that if the parents think it is teatime, so everyone should sit down and eat the same food, then this is for the family good. Often, tidying up or chores is an area in which this conventional wisdom operates very strongly, but as with so much, it needs questioning.

Fifteen-year-old Siobhan lives with her mum (a sculptor), her dad (a therapist), ten-year-old brother Eamon and sister Caitlin (aged six). Her parents are trying to live by consent, but they have an ingrained idea that the family has a form of contract to one another and should each do their share of chores. Caitlin has quickly learned to take advantage of her status as the youngest to avoid compulsion, but Eamon and Siobhan seem to be in constant conflict about chores. Sometimes they will spontaneously join in with polishing or vacuuming, but they resent being pulled away from watching TV or doing something they enjoy to do particular tasks at particular times. The parents see this resentment as intransigence and irrationality, but Siobhan has some counter arguments. She points out that her mother's attic studio is always messy, so surely her mother can see that tidiness is not essential always and everywhere; rather it is a matter of such things as function, taste and individual comfort level. Siobhan points out that the reason for having a pristine hallway and stairs is that her father's clients come through that way to reach his therapy room. Not all children live in homes with this kind of dual use, and it is not her responsibility to provide a work environment for her father. She argues that she did not consent to being born and does not feel that she has actually had a choice about entering into any contract with her parents. Siobhan says that she is quite happy with a certain level of mess. It is her mother and father who have the highest standards and comfort requirements, so they should find ways of getting their needs met that do not involve forcing chores on her and Eamon.

Siobhan also points out that the reason that they can't ever find a solution, but simply go round and round in circles, is that they don't even have the same problem. Her parents' problem is how to keep the house clean. Since they have an idea about a necessary level of tidiness, they constantly look for any mess and focus on this. Siobhan's (and Eamon's) problem is that they feel very unhappy when their parents clearly disapprove of them, but also feel unhappy when they are made to do things against their will. The children want both parental approval and to be able to spend time on the things that are important to them, but it seems that these two things are constantly put in opposition to one another. Siobhan suggests that she would be happy to help her parents solve their problem and asks that they help her with her problems, too.

Having identified the problems, Siobhan and her parents finally set about looking for solutions. Lots of suggestions are made. They could hire someone to come in and clean the house. Siobhan's father says he doesn't like the idea of a stranger in his therapy room where he keeps confidential records. Siobhan suggests a locked cabinet. Eamon says he doesn't think there are enough bins and laundry baskets in the house. Caitlin adds that her friends have a lot more machines in their kitchen, like a dishwasher and microwave. Mum says that she is constantly uneasy with strangers coming and going in the house and feels under pressure to have a home that will please these strangers. She suggests that they dig out the plans they had for an extension to the side of the house so that the therapy practice would not intrude on their home and she wouldn't feel so anxious about tidiness. This would also give space for Siobhan and Caitlin to have their own rooms, which would solve other problems. Everyone talks about the household chores that they enjoy even occasionally. They agree that those things that no one likes or which no one would enjoy regularly should be the things they pay for help with.

If everyone were happy, the discussion might end there, with recognition that no one within the family should be put in a position where they feel either compelled or disapproved of. However, a new problem might be thrown up by the solutions that have been offered. Eamon might ask how much these solutions are going to cost and wonder whether paying for all this will mean putting off the purchase of a computer he has been longing for. This might lead to prioritizing the solutions or refining them or even to going back to the original problem and questioning the assumption that the house needs to be as tidy as the parents first suggested. The family will keep going until they have a genuine mutual solution because it is spurious to assert that the good of the group sometimes has to take precedence over the good and happiness of anyone in the group. The group is made up of the family members. If one of them is unhappy, then the good of the group is harmed too, no matter how much it is pretended otherwise.

- The good of the family group is not served unless all the individuals in the group are happy.
- Our children did not sign a contract with us before they were born to agree to taking on a share of the domestic work.
- Children may be quite happy to help parents find the level of tidiness they feel comfortable with, but they should not be compelled into meeting their parents' needs.
- Children's own space is just that. They may welcome help, suggestions and storage solutions to keep their possessions in order and undamaged, but they may simply have very different comfort levels than our own.

Sex, drugs and who knows what

For many, consent seeking stops here, but, will compulsion work? The prospect of our children becoming sexually active and vulnerable is one that fills most parents with fear. Despite this, it is going to happen. At some point our children are going to begin exploring their own sexuality. Our choice is whether they do so armed with lots of good quality, none scare-mongering information and in the complete knowledge that they can come to us as trusted advisors or whether they go into relationships ignorant of anything except rumor and dubious folk-lore. Parents can only keep the doors locked for so many hours of the day and the damage that can be done by seeking to control the basic human sex drive of another person is unfathomable. Of course we have morality, opinions, experience and access to information about health, risks, social mores and attitudes. We should share all of this, but we should not imagine that compulsion is going to be any more moral or useful in this arena than any other.

As with sex, the issue of drugs is a vexed area that fills parents with fear. Having access to high quality information and trusted advice is ultimately much better protection and a far superior basis for reasonable and self fulfilling (not self destructive) decisions. This is, after all, an arena where simply laying down the law has had a history of tragic failure.

- We should share moral ideas and copious information with our children and trust that they will make reasonable decisions that are in their own best interests.
- Children grow up and have to make complex decisions, but they are best placed to do so when their parents are trusted advisors to whom they can turn.

But sometimes…

As I argued at the beginning of this chapter, "What if…?" is the wrong question. It presumes that children are innately anti-social and self destructive, but they are not. The more children are treated as rational, resourceful, complete people the more an environment of consent and problem solving is built. It is all too easy to think that the issues that concern us are universal, but the truth is that even the most authoritarian parents don't generally agree on what areas of life are so important that they require compulsion.

I recently spent time with a family who had strict ideas about sugar consumption, bedtime, the importance of homework and a whole long list of other 'essentials'. Yet the same family was very relaxed about alcohol consumption by young teenagers. The so called 'important' or 'essential' areas that are too momentous to take chances with are simply not agreed upon by parents at large and this might be an indication that these things are not as obvious as is often imagined. That said, there are a very few extreme circumstances where the level of agreement rises sharply, perhaps indicating memes that have been particularly useful and which have survived for a reason.

The most obvious is perhaps the oft-cited speeding truck. We don't think it reasonable to leave our four year old in the path of an oncoming juggernaut simply because we know that she wanted to see her friend across the street. We actually know in this situation that the child is not suicidal and would be much happier to cross the road safely given the chance. We may not be mind readers, but this is a guess that is more than likely going to work out for us and in any case the alternative of not scooping our child up is too horrible to contemplate.

Some emergencies demand that we take action without first reaching any consent. In such rare situations we have to guess that the consent would be given. However, we also have to be wary of using this logic on more than a handful of occasions in any lifetime. It is exactly the kind of logic that non consent seeking parents use. It's not uncommon to hear a conventional parent holding down a child to have his teeth brushed by force and claiming that the child will thank him later. This is exactly the kind of thinking that lies behind parental decisions to act for a child's so called 'own good' or 'best interests' even against her will. It is not, therefore, something that should be a normal part of the thinking of consent seeking parents, yet sometimes it will arise. When?

Consent seeking is not about blue-prints and definitive lists. Nurturing our children's independence is a complex and subtle process. What we can say, however, is that certain strong memes seem to be held, if not universally, then with overwhelming assent amongst free thinking people. On this basis we can tentatively say that on rare occasions when we fail to find mutual solutions, when parental self surrender will do nothing to help the child then and when our best guess is that we can presume consent, other things being equal, then we have to act accordingly. Obvious examples would be:

- Occasions when there is simply no time to find explicit consent; a child running into the path of a lorry or jumping from a high window.
- Occasions when a medical emergency does not allow the normal processes of problem solving and we know our child wants to live.

Such thinking would also extend to those vanishingly rare occasions when we have to step in to prevent something (or at least not assist an action) that is overwhelmingly agreed upon as harmful, examples would be:

- Preventing a six year old engaging in a sexual relationship with an adult.
- Preventing a child wanting from murdering or injuring his best friend after a quarrel.
- Preventing a child determined to destroy someone else's property

This kind of thinking, where consent is not found in the short term should not be commonplace or routine, in fact for most children it may never arise at all. Nor is this the end of the process; we should still go on seeking consent and not use a hard case to justify sliding back into compulsion and authority. We certainly should not use such rare and extreme cases to reason that:

- We have to compel a child to brush her teeth because she will appreciate it when she's an adult.
- We have to limit TV now because little Jimmy will thank us when he's a brain surgeon not a couch potato.

It needs to be born in mind that:

- Emergencies of time, danger or overwhelming moral compulsion are rare.
- If you find yourself confronting such emergencies more than once or twice in the life time of most children then you are probably letting this thinking invade your relationship and you may need to re-think your consent seeking.

- A possible check is to think about whether there is a strong meme held by the vast majority of free thinking people in this area; the more disagreement you find, the more likely it is that you don't need to resort to emergency behavior.
- The process of finding mutual solutions should still be used; you can't have a discussion with a comatose child, but you can keep communicating with a child bent on murder and work on changing her theories
- Remember that the real question is why would a child who has been nurtured, fully engaged with and treated as both reasonable and self-fulfilling suddenly engage in anti- social or self-destructive behavior?

What Will People Think?

Dealing with other people's opinions of our parenting is a real concern for parents, but such concerns do not have to prevent us from living consensually with our children. One of the things that often impede us most in the area of finding mutual solutions is that adults, particularly parents, often seem to be inflicted with an excruciating urge to appease complete strangers, even if it means sabotaging our child's autonomy and freedom of thought. When eleven-year-old twins, Jessica and Louise, are out shopping at the supermarket their mother finds it terribly embarrassing that the girls skip along the aisles singing a chorus of 'knickers, bras and pants' as they go. Her embarrassment is like a beacon and the more she looks uncomfortable and tries to shush the girls, the more strangers seem to shoot her disapproving glances or cluck their tongues loudly. However, when the girls go shopping with their Grandma the next week and repeat their performance, Grandma merely smiles or winks at the passing strangers and feels sure that they think her grand daughters just as amusing and delightful as she does.

A great deal of what we assume that other people are thinking about our children and about us is in our own imaginations. The more relaxed we are about going on the bus with our magenta haired fifteen-year-old or going to the cinema with our six-year-old in a batman suit, the more likely people are to respond positively or hardly to notice. Even if other people do respond negatively to something our child says or does, our primary role is as the child's parent, trusted advisor and helper, not as an apologist for conventional memes or views on children. Children are independent people and, with a lot of input and assistance, treating them as such both protects their personal domain and gives us, the parents, the best possible role. We don't have to apologize for such parenting.

Having said that, it can be good idea to politely, sweetly, but firmly dispel any myths about consent-based parenting that might feed others' cause for concern. Giving your child freedom and helping him to get what he wants is not the same as abandoning him to his own devices; neglected children have little or no trusted adult input into their lives and very few, if any, moral ideas available to them, which is certainly not true of our children. You can let interested people know that our children have a lot of input, conversation, information and moral ideas shared with them; our children are not raising themselves, they are simply having their humanity nurtured. Consent based parenting is not about control, but that does not make it an 'anything goes' style of parenting, rather it enables children to develop their inner motivation and control. When consent is working well, self interest and morality go hand in hand.

- Constantly worrying about what other people think is a recipe for paralysis, not parenting.
- Children are much more important than the opinion of strangers, though this needn't entail conflict; humor, reasonableness and confidence can go a long way.
- For the most part we won't need to justify our parenting, but where a discussion arises we can be very clear that finding consent is not about neglect or any lack of sharing moral ideas.

Parenting is so much more satisfying when we are not in constant conflict with the people we care for most. Sometimes, overwhelmed or under pressure, parents sadly opt for a 'quiet life' by backing out of their children's lives and leaving them to get on with it, but that kind of 'quiet life' generally catches up with parents when their neglected offspring run into serious problems. Parenting simply is a big task and if we are not happy with neglect, as few parents are, then we have to decide what kind of involvement with our children we will have; will it be authoritarian, compulsion-based parenting with all the conflict entailed or will it be about seeking consent and mutual solutions?

I am convinced that compulsion is wrong; that it harms our relationships and our ability to think clearly. I don't believe that I have the right to sabotage another's independence because I'm older or have more experience (much of it of dubious quality anyway) or even because I love my children. When we think like this then we start to focus on win-win relationship cycles and these in turn breed more win-win solutions. This type of parenting isn't simple, it demands resourcefulness and reasonableness and creating new ideas within our families. Compulsion isn't simple either; it takes endless energy and stress to try to control someone else's life. The truth is that no parenting style is simple; the choice is simply about how we spend our energy.

9
Will They Ever Learn?

"Education, education, education" are the buzzwords of our time. Parents generally want to do the best that they can for their children and this usually involves providing them with the best possible education. For many people the idea that we can live by consent breaks down at this point. The concern is that children who are accustomed to having their preferences met are surely going to suffer educationally; they simply won't be the kind of children who are prepared to fit into the school environment, they won't get up to go to school on time, won't adhere to the school rules and won't cope with requirements for hard work and homework. The assumption is that a great deal of education rests on some level of compulsion, and that children used to getting what they want are going to find this difficult, if not impossible.

As you might guess by now the motto of finding consent is 'question everything' and the same is true when it comes to education and schooling.

Taught a Lesson

Conventional wisdom maintains that children have to be systematically given formal instruction for years in order to learn, yet around ninety thousand children educated at home in the United Kingdom and over a million home based educators in the United States are consistently demonstrating that this is simply not the case. Of course not everyone who wants to remove compulsion from their child's life and live by consent will be a home educator. Children who are used to being treated with respect can thrive in any environment provided it meets their own ends, but the existence of home education serves as a clear demonstration that learning does not have to rely on the kind of school teaching that we normally imagine is essential.

The best learning occurs when it matches our inner motivation and this is the case whether a child is in school because this suits her purposes or is learning at home in any one of a number of innovative styles from structured courses to unstructured conversations or play. Meeting our preferences is a powerful educational tool; we learn best the things we want to know and that is true in or out of school.

Autonomy is the right of self-government and free will. Education is the process by which we develop intellectual potential and foster the growth of new ideas. The best education occurs when our inner goals and the leaning environment come together. Compulsion doesn't assist real learning any more than it assists children to become rational decision makers.

Once we have begun the process of finding mutual solutions with our children, then the subject of whether to go to school or not is bound to arise. Some children choose to go to school, just as some choose to make use of authoritarian youth organizations or other groups and institutions which happen to be offering opportunities and experiences which meet their preferences at the time. You don't have to abandon schools in order to live by consent with your child and promote her real learning, but it should be an option, depending on the mutual solutions of the family.

Children are natural learners; born as reasonable, creative thinkers with unimpaired minds. Parents (and other trusted adults) have an enormous role to play in helping children to achieve their goals and in introducing children to a wide range of possible interests. The best learning occurs when the child wants to know for her own ends and the adult helpers engage with this motivation to contribute to the learning.

Let's take Jasmine. Like most children Jasmine starts out as an enquiring, curious child who loves to be read to, learns nursery rhymes and colors, enjoys counting chocolate buttons (and subtracting them) and playing endlessly. At four, Jasmine joins the reception class at the local primary school. At first she is quite happy. She likes the teacher and enjoys the activities; largely playing, drawing and dressing up. She does get rather tired and grumpy quite often, but everyone tells Jasmine's Mum, Nina, that this is quite normal and Jasmine never says that she doesn't want to go to school.

A year goes by without incident and Jasmine returns to year one of primary school the next autumn. Suddenly life is much more formal and the school day is longer. Within a couple of weeks Jasmine is not a sunny, inquisitive little girl, but a frequently distressed child who Nina finds uncommunicative and aggressive by turn. Talking to Jasmine's class teacher, Nina discovers that Jasmine is already being labeled as 'slow'. Apparently Jasmine never seems to hear whole class instructions, simply doesn't complete much of the set worksheets and seems switched off and remote. In the playground Jasmine starts to report being bullied, but Jasmine's teacher informs Nina that Jasmine makes herself a victim by being 'odd' and that this really can't be called bullying, despite the broken spectacles and the accumulation of bruises. When Nina persists with her complaints, the school principal decides to have Jasmine assessed; perhaps Jasmine is a little deaf he suggests or perhaps she has some problem like Asperger's Syndrome.

Reluctantly, Nina decides to withdraw Jasmine from school and educate her at home. At first Nina tries to replicate what she thinks school should be about, but her life with Jasmine becomes a battleground and Jasmine's resistance and distress seem to increase daily. Defeated, Nina decides that Jasmine needs a period of readjustment and they begin to take life more easily. Jasmine watches TV programs that generate a lot of discussion and sometimes get followed up with library visits or projects. They go to social meetings with other home educating families and sometimes join in with activities or trips organized by the group. They spend lots of time in a park that has a woodland adventure playground and a small wildlife area where animals are rehabilitated after injuries. Jasmine also starts to learn the violin and does a lot of drawing and model making. As both Nina and Jasmine relax, Jasmine becomes inquisitive and motivated again, though the pattern of her learning is much more like the flexible pre-school years than anything that could be observed in school.

As Jasmine grows she develops her own interests more and more. She builds models from everything available, spends lots of time on the Internet, plays computer games, plays her violin, sometimes keeps a journal, draws and paints, watches masses of documentaries on nature and science, follows some favorite TV series avidly, becoming familiar with the scripts and character development, watches virtually any movie available and reads some science fantasy.

By the time Jasmine is fourteen Nina secretly worries that her daughter's education is unbalanced and odd and she is concerned about Jasmine's level of spelling and writing ability. Nina doesn't mention this, but keeps supporting Jasmine to follow her own interests. A year later, after some discussions following a TV show, Jasmine decides she wants to sign up to do a formal course in English with a distance learning college. Nina is worried that at fifteen and with no background of formal study or essay writing Jasmine will flounder, but Jasmine's interest is strong and she enjoys the course, adding courses in sociology and politics a year later.

At eighteen Jasmine is offered a place at university to do an English and journalism degree, but that summer she meets a photographer who is doing a PhD on the social meanings of color and she decides to go touring the world with him. Jasmine returns a year later, alone, but with sheaves of notes, photographs and drawings and tells Nina that she plans to make some money designing websites to support herself while she writes and illustrates a science fantasy book for children about a parallel universe without color. In order to write the book, Jasmine decides she needs to talk to some physicists about the theory of parallel universes and so she meets and falls in love with Gary, a PhD graduate in his first university lecturing post.

Gary introduces Jasmine to lots of new ideas and also re-awakens her old love of computer games and a new love of math that she has virtually never studied before. Jasmine finds a publisher for her book and keeps up her website design to make a living, but spends more and more time doing math courses, especially the kind that relate to computer programming for games. With her skills in graphics and her flair for plot and drama, Jasmine talks her way into a job in a small, innovative computer game design firm and Nina finally relaxes.

Ironically, Jasmine, who, despite her own unusual education, has not thrown off the conventional ideas about learning, notices that her own little girl, Amelia, seems to be struggling in her six year old math class. Jasmine worries anxiously that Amelia's options in life will be restricted unless she gets to grips with math, but luckily Gary has been talking to Nina. He wants to give up lecturing, and thinks they should home educate Amelia, trusting that her inner motivation and curiosity will see her through.

- The single most important factor in learning is motivation. Whether a child chooses home or school, structured courses or the most unlikely combination of interests (some of which aren't traditionally called 'education' at all) it is the desire to learn that makes the difference.
- Most families choose school as the route to education, but an increasing number do not and when we begin living by consent this is another area to re-asses.

You Live and You Learn

All of life is for learning and when a family begins to live by consent all of life changes; decisions about school, arbitrary rules about such things as bedtime, food, dress code and chores are all re-assessed, but one area that often remains particularly hard to think innovatively about is the use of any media with a screen.

In order to value all learning and to foster independence we have to let go of artificial definitions of what is 'educational' and 'not educational'. As soon as we begin to construct a hierarchical value system in which reading a book is more approved of than watching a soap opera; doing a math problem is more worthy than lying on the sofa gazing into space then we are interfering with what is going on in someone else's mind. Moreover, these judgments about the learning taking place in someone else's mind can damage the process of inner motivation which is at the core of independent learning. Erasing the lines of demarcation between 'education' and 'not education' is a far reaching and liberating step, especially when it comes to the vexed area of children's use of television, computers and screen-based games.

TV and computer games are commonly accused of making children violent, yet they are just as frequently blamed for turning children into passive couch potatoes. I want to suggest that screen media are nothing more than tools. They are neither surrogate parents justifying neglect nor demonic forces controlling children against their wills. Of course, parents might be forgiven for being momentarily taken in by other arguments when there are so many voices raised.

Most of us are happy for children to remain in control whilst they are choosing reading or math or history activities or whilst they are viewing specifically educational TV, using CD ROMs marketed for their educational content or building Lego models. However, fewer parents can see the value of self-direction when their child becomes fascinated by a particular soap opera, watches every action movie made or plays CD ROMs full of strategy and fantasy violence. It is much more common to assume that such material is not only 'not educational', but actively damaging to children's creativity and even to their morality or ability to think for themselves.

Faced with theories that TV or computer games cause bad behavior or reduce children to zombie like states of suggestibility, many parents wonder if the trade off between a little compulsion and increased protection is a good one. So what are parents to do?

The first step is to go back to fundamental memes. In Chapter 5 we questioned the idea that anything we like, enjoy and find wholly entertaining must be bad for us. When it comes to TV and computer games this idea has run riot and we are easily convinced that these media, which so many children enjoy, are very bad indeed, including being:

- Addictive.
- Destructive of creativity and thinking.
- Liable to create lethargy or increase aggression (or even, despite the contradiction, both)
- The source of irresistible bad or inappropriate ideas.

Parents who are influenced by these ideas have plenty of company. There is a plethora of so-called 'evidence' (though it rarely deserves the name) linking TV, for instance, to violent behavior in children. Writing in the *New York Times* Denise Caruso says,

"Hundreds of studies in recent decades have revealed a direct correlation between exposure to media violence -- now including video games -- and increased aggression."

She links TV and games with, "psychological techniques of desensitization, conditioning and vicarious learning" and adds that a number of young killers such as Michael Carneal, the 14-year-old boy who opened fire on a prayer group in a school foyer in 1997, and the boys who conducted the massacre at Littleton Colorado, were accomplished games players. However, she entirely fails to set out any logical process of cause and effect. Correlation is simply not the same as cause, as we can see more clearly when we consider that there is a huge correlation between increased ice cream sales in Britain and increased levels of drowning. Caruso sites Joel Federman, co-director of the Center for Communication and Social Policy at the University of California at Santa Barbara, as her expert witness. Yet Federman, author of *The Social Effects of Interactive Electronic Games*, acknowledges that studies have been limited and do not agree. He has to admit,

" ... since not every kid experiences the extreme effects, people can continue to deny them." (Copyright 1999 The New York Times Company)

This is precisely the point of the counter argument. We have some correlation, perhaps, but that does not add up to cause. What is it in the life of the children who go on to offend or even kill that is the common causative thread? The truth is that it is extremely hard to know, but the argument that the common thread is not TV or computer games, but compulsion and/or neglect is certainly credible. If we systematically destroy a child's ability to think reasonably and control his own life and learning then it should hardly seem surprising that antisocial and violent behaviors result. Children who kill, become violent or are switched off from life are highly damaged individuals, alienated from themselves, their peers and their communities. It is simplistic and unsupportable to blame a computer strategy game, an action movie or graphic song lyrics.

Television is an object. It is a source of learning in so many areas of thinking. It delivers information quickly and in a form that is eminently digestible. Video games provide stimulating entertainment and build up a vast store of knowledge about problem solving. We don't have to be suspicious of these tools if we take some time to tackle the memes that demonize them.

Firstly, liking something is not a warning sign of addiction. Addiction is a much over used word and one that would be unlikely to leap to mind if our child spent ten hours a day at the piano or learning chess. In fact, we tend to like things that we are learning from, so, far from being a sign of danger, liking something is a good sign. We have to stop thinking that if something is fun it must be bad and begin to value enjoyment.

Neither is TV liking destructive of creativity and thought. We know from general experience that a great deal of learning is inexplicit. We are often not consciously aware of the learning taking place in our minds and certainly not immediately, so to presume that we can neatly divide the world up into 'learning' and 'non learning' experience is nonsense. Given that we can't have privileged access to other minds or second guess learning at every stage, we have to proceed very cautiously, before we damn something as 'rubbish' or 'useless' to another person. What we can observe is whether or not a child is motivated to pursue an activity; whether it is an activity that the child values and enjoys. I want to suggest that motivation and enjoyment are actually very good indicators that thinking and learning are taking place.

Using enjoyment or 'fun' as an educational indicator takes seriously that a lot of what we learn in life doesn't come from formal study, but from all kinds of unexpected places in a huge variety of ways, many of them building up inexplicitly, but deeply valuable for our learning. In a culture that has become pre-occupied with a tick box approach to learning it is easy to assume that a math lecture is always going to be more educational than doing something we explicitly enjoy (like watching a TV show or playing a video game). Is this the truth or is it because we have taken on false ideas that tell us that learning is about hard work and endurance, whilst fun is just the self indulgent froth of life that does us no good? In other words our obsession with measuring learning may have blinded us to the huge variety of learning that a person needs in a life time, much of it not measurable at all.

When we actually stop to think about it, we know that a not only is a lot of our learning inexplicit, but that a huge amount of knowledge is not readily susceptible to tests and measures, We also know that the things we want to learn and enjoy the most are the things that tend to stay with us long after we have forgotten everything we crammed into our short-term memory for tests and exams.

There is a lot more to learning and personal development than what can be tested on the surface and the learning that lasts tends to be in areas where preferences, self fulfillment, delight and interest are uppermost. If this is so, then video games and enjoyable TV programs should be seen not as threats to children's thinking, but as innovative and creative learning tools. Creative people need stimulation and TV and computer games, as well as books and conversation, provide excellent stimulation, allowing new ideas to flourish. What's more they do so cheaply and, in the case of video games, with the added stimulation of interaction, which is generally acknowledged to be an essential element in creativity.

It is not TV or video games that create lethargy or increase aggression in children, but systematic compulsion or appalling neglect. What leads us to believe that TV is a culprit is that, sadly, many neglected children have nothing but TV or video games to turn to. These children do not have access to conversation, moral input or other stimulating contexts. This is a far cry from blaming TV; a child left with only an electric toaster for company and entertainment might also withdraw or become aggressive, but we would not blame the toaster. We do not have to fear the supposed 'aggression' of things like computer games. In reality no one gets hurt in a game, the objects involved are 2D images and, like adults, children are well accustomed to the dramatic technique of opposing good and bad forces in every other sphere of fictional life. Plays and novels all use such dramatic tension, but we don't worry that our children will emulate the murders in Shakespearean plays or imitate the rapes played out in books such as Margaret Attwood's 'The Handmaid's Tale' or Anthony Burgess' 'Clockwork Orange' (both compulsory set texts in the current English A level syllabus in Britain for 16-18 year olds).

What about the supposed links with lethargy? Let's take Christine. Christine is convinced that her tendency to be 'lazy' comes from being brought up in home where the TV was permanently on and where TV was her parent's main priority. Christine therefore feels strongly that TV would damage her children's ability to think and be motivated and so she restricts Natalie (14) and Edward's (11) viewing. Christine's cousin, Julie, grew up in a very similar home. Julie disputes that it was TV that made Christine lazy and points out that although her own childhood was similar, she herself became academically industrious and tried to be as different as possible from her parents. In neither case, Julie argues, was the television the cause of laziness or academic industry. In both cases, parental neglect, and individual reactions to it had effects on the cousins' different thinking.

Christine is not convinced; as well as fearing that her children will become lazy and sluggish if they are allowed to watch 'too much' TV she also persists with the idea that her children might 'copy' bad behavior from television programs. Christine argues that she has observed tendencies of this in Natalie and Edward. She tells Julie that after a couple of hours of TV viewing her children sometimes go into a state of 'zombification', whilst at other times they are wound up with excessive energy. Julie points out that this observation is not objective and value neutral and that Christine's tight restrictions on viewing and her overt disapproval of anything with the merest hint of violence are also part of the context. Christine cannot be argued with, but she does secretly wonder about Julie's children, Petra (13), Kaye (10) and Daniel (8). They have no viewing restrictions; all have their own televisions and video players and seem to have periods when they watch a lot of television and times when they do not. There is always a lot of lively conversation in Julie's house, often on a breadth of topics that Natalie and Edward seem uninterested in and Christine cannot honestly say that she observes any of the 'zombification' or swings of aggression in her cousin's children that her own children exhibit.

What is different? Quite simply, it is compulsion. Television is a neutral object, but imposing restrictions around its use causes irrationality. Denying someone access to the information, ideas and entertainment that television provides cuts off a whole arena of motivated learning. It can never be for the child's own good for a parent to take away a child's ability to think for herself, nor to behave as thought the child is too irrational or stupid to make her own decisions.

TV and game playing do not perpetrate bad ideas that are hard to resist. This is not to say that every idea presented on TV, whether it comes in a documentary, a soap, a sit-com or an advert, is a good idea. The ideas presented are variously good, bad, constructive, and destructive and every other kind of human idea, but children don't learn to challenge and sift ideas if they are prevented from engaging with them. Television is a diverse source of cheap and easily accessed information. Moreover, it is a deeply effective medium for communicating culture.

Fears about a child watching 'inappropriate material' (usually anything which is deemed to have a sexual or violent content) are simply based on asking the wrong question. How do we go from assuming that children are born innately reasonable, trustworthy and good to believing that if given a TV they will instantly become irrational, self-destructive and bad? Children in consent seeking homes will choose to watch the things which further the learning that only they know is going on in their own minds. They will choose content which has meaning to them, which helps them explore the questions they are ready to explore, which can be safely and fruitfully followed up in conversations with parents and other trusted adults.

- TV and video games are not addictive, merely activities that many children enjoy to greater or lesser extents; enjoyment is a good sign.

- TV and video games are not destructive of creativity and thinking, but can be instrumental in aiding creativity and learning.
- TV and video games are not liable to create lethargy or increase aggression. Research to the contrary is poorly done, contradictory and fails to take account for complex factors in children's real contexts.
- TV and video games do not perpetrate ideas that are hard to resist. These mediums expose children to every kind of idea, many excellent and many appalling, and it is this exposure to ideas together with a context of engagement and conversation that helps children to reach good ideas of their own.

The Proof of the Pudding

Children are not products that are improved by using the best recipe. Parenting, like all activities involving human relationship, is unpredictable and risky. We have to forget the pseudo science of testing parenting theories for results and instead decide on whether we are willing to take a moral and reasoned approach to parenting and trust that the spin offs will be equally moral and reasoned, even if they might also be full of surprises.

One of the key characteristics of making a switch from conventional to consent based parenting is the movement away from predicting or prescribing outcomes for our children. Authoritarian parents tend to have very clear pictures of the kinds of people they want and expect their children to become. The ideal may include attributes like godliness, respect for authority, selflessness, and industriousness etc. More liberal parents, on the other hand, may have hopes for revolutionary free-thinkers. Those between these extremes may have more amorphous aims in mind, perhaps wanting their children to become rounded or responsible adults. Naturally we all want our children to be happy and to be able to do the things they want in life, but this is a far cry from making predictions or encouraging parents to look for outcomes in children.

The problem with thinking about children as products is that a product has to meet certain standards and criteria before it can be acceptable. All too often this results in children who do not meet the required standard being labeled. The labeling might be judgmental and intended to shame: Frank is a naughty child; Aislin is such a willful, stubborn little girl; Savita is a selfish little so and so. Alternatively, it might be the kind of labeling which categorizes children according to the growing plethora of 'syndromes', as I discussed in Chapter 4. Labeling a child all too neatly accounts for her faultiness without ever needing to question whether she is simply a distressed human being who is not getting what she wants from life.

We need to remember that what we see of another person is only what is visible at that time. It is a small snapshot of a process, not a static definition. Our children are not products. The point is to help the individual child live his own life by his own lights in the way that most pleases him, not to mold him into a new set of attributes which seem more functional and pleasing to parents. This is true, even when the molding is dressed up in the insidious cloak of being for the child's 'own good'.

Such thinking seems counter cultural at the moment because currently state education systems are very keen to view our children as products. In school children become viewed as raw materials to which we add another high value raw material, namely education. With the mixture of the base product (child) and the value added product (education) we have a final product (civilized or functional young person). Whether our children attend school or are educated at home, we need to move away from such thinking which reduces human beings and their relations to inputs and outputs.

Thinking of children as products also gives the false impression that we can experimentally test parenting theories, but this is not so. Consent based living stands or falls on the truths that underpin it. If you see all humans as unique, morally responsible, thinking and creative, as well as fallible, then consent based living is simply the right way to live and we can expect its spin-offs to be good, even if we can't predict outcomes or describe the perfect child.

- Children are people, not products.
- Offering information and observations should stop short of molding children into pre-defined outcomes.
- Helping our children to get what they want from life now is infinitely more valuable and moral than trying to ensure that a child becomes a particular kind of person.
- None of this means that finding mutual solutions with children should result in disaster. The spin offs of good parenting should be good, but outcomes cannot be predicted or controlled.

10
In the Real World

Real life is full of real problems. Without recourse to compulsion, parents often feel at a loss as to how to negotiate what seem like intractable problems or matters of emergency. We know that the real world isn't about to hand us what you want on a plate, so we assume that getting what we want as children will only lead to unrealistic expectations, disappointment, and an inability to fit in. But will it?

First, it's worth remembering that children who are used to finding solutions live in a world just as real as children who are used to being forced to do things and whose decisions are over-ridden. Making children do what adults want of them is a common cultural convenience. It is routine to hear parents saying things like, 'You have to put your coat on and leave playing right this second because I have to be somewhere.' We assume that we have no alternative to compulsion in many everyday situations with children. Yet it would be unthinkable to behave like this in the wider world amongst adults.

We don't negotiate a loan by telling the lender that he has no choice but to give us the money right now because it's important; we have to convince him that there is a good reason to lend the money. We don't demand that our dentist makes time to see us for a non-emergency appointment right this minute in order to fit it in with our shopping trip; we expect her to make an appointment at a mutually convenient time. We are quite used to a vast range of interactions in the real world that require that we negotiate mutually convenient solutions. We do it all the time without giving it a second thought; it is merely polite, ordinary behavior, yet we simultaneously convince ourselves that it would be unthinkable or even impossible to do the same with our own children.

Why? Not because of any inherent or special difficulties in this kind of negotiation. In fact in many instances negotiating with people we know very well and who we share familial bonds with is easier than negotiating with bank managers and medical professionals. Once again bad ideas have convinced us that children are irrational, untrustworthy or even purposefully trying to make our lives as difficult as possible, but if we question these ideas then it is easier to appreciate that there is no reason why a child shouldn't be interested in finding mutual solutions. Similarly, there is no good reason why children shouldn't be able to understand genuine emergencies when the discussion has to come later. Solutions are out there, but we don't always find them and sometimes this is simply because we don't have ways of thinking about them.

Do you remember Paula and her children Zoë and Jacob? Zoë, at seven, was able to respond positively to a real emergency when her baby brother's life was in danger and Paula needed to get to the hospital immediately and without discussion. Zoë knew that her mother would not tell her something was too urgent to discuss unless it was the truth, because Paula had not spent the previous seven years using force on Zoë just to get the weekly shopping done.

The question often persists:
Does all of this emphasis on winning simply give children a false notion of what the world is like?

We don't behave like this in other spheres. It is not reasonable for a bank-manager to arbitrarily refuse loans to some customers to teach some people what deprivation is like and toughen them up. Life presents us with real complex problems at all ages. We get enough practice in problem solving through real events without resorting to artificial lessons 'just in case.'

Learning that it is possible to negotiate mutual solutions and that open mindedness, resourcefulness and the ability to review our ideas leads to good solutions is an excellent way of finding such solutions both now and in later life. People who expect to lose often go on losing, perpetuating the same cycle of disempowerment that hampered them as children. Children who are helped to win in everyday situations do not expect that they will never have to solve problems or that life will be handed to them on a plate. What they do learn is that although problem solving is sometimes difficult, none the less it is possible, especially when they have the flexibility to appreciate that change and risk are part of the equation. What they do not do is conflate problems with suffering or effort with sacrifice.

- We are born with reason and we learn to use it best when we are accustomed to a lifetime of being treated as reasoning, creative, resourceful people.
- Having our reason nurtured is more likely to promote solutions than following artificial rules.
- Your child won't be disabled from negotiating real problems because of a history of successfully finding solutions, but he could be chronically disabled from following all kinds of paths if he isn't assisted to solve his current problems now using reason and resourcefulness, however trivial these problems might appear.

- Life contains enough real problems, risks and challenges without manufacturing hardships. If we help our children to find solutions to real problems now they will go on solving real problems throughout life.

Finding Consent with Limited Resources

Most of our problems come down to our ideas; especially when our ideas are skewed or limited. In a culture in which the convenience of adults is rated more highly than taking children into consideration, it is all too easy to slip into family patterns in which we assume things have to be a certain way. We say things like, 'I have to do the dishes now' as though the universe would break down if we did not or, even worse, we attribute needs to inanimate objects. 'The carpet needs vacuuming' is clearly nonsense; carpets don't have needs and our preference for clean carpets is not part of the fabric of the universe. Of course, there are real laws of physics; we can't fly unaided, though we can go a long way to simulating safe experiences of flight in all kinds of ways. It is also true that we are fallible and limited. We will not always find solutions and nor am I suggesting that parents are obligated to go to unlimited lengths on every given occasion. Your child may want her very own space rocket, but it is likely that you don't have the resources of NASA and aren't morally obligated to provide a space rocket. You can, however, still work on finding a mutually preferred outcome to the child's problem. None of us have endless money; all of us live in real time with only twenty-four hours in a day. Often compulsion arises because of these simple, shared limitations, no matter how much we'd like to reach consent, but does this have to be so?

Learning to win and getting what we want are not the same as a child having everything at the snap of his fingers, but neither should parents assume that there are resources over which they have no control to help their children. This is particularly the case with budget constraints or limited time. We don't have to be rich to live by consent, but we do have to be resourceful. Learning to win is a matter of creatively finding solutions. This will certainly lead to very new ways of considering and using family budgets, but it does not lead to bankruptcy. Moreover, things actually acquired may look very different from any initial wish list.

Many times, conventional parents tell children that they cannot afford a particular wanted item when the truth is that it is simply not their priority. If we are going to live by consent then there must be some basic honesty and openness about family finances. Is more being spent on fuel bills than is necessary simply because the parents haven't researched alternative suppliers? Does the 'essential' food bill include regular adult 'take-away' food when the children are told that take-away pizza is unaffordable? Do the children agree that expensive furniture and new clothes are vital, whilst extra televisions for family members are out of reach? Would the children rather use the money from piano classes for a year on a trip to Disney land or vice versa? The questions and answers will be endlessly various between different families. The point is simply that everything can be questioned.

Twelve-year-old twins, Leila and Arun, would like to have more technology available. There is often too much competition for the family's one television and, under the previous family regime, they were often expected to give way to their little brother, Nanik (aged six). Arun would like more opportunities to explore the Internet and design web sites, but the one family computer is over-subscribed and his fathers' work takes precedence. Arun has watched the Discovery channel at a friend's house and would also like a television with a cable connection. Leila loves movies and would like a video to go with a television in her own room. Nanik adds that he would like to have the cable cartoon channel and a Play Station. The family sits down and talks about the wish list, at which point Mum adds that she would like access to the movie channels and Dad says he would like a more modern computer with specifications more suited to his current work.

The family is not rich and the wish list involves money. Dad suggests he could take on an extra freelance contract for a limited time or Mum could do some agency nursing (her former career). Nanik says he doesn't like it when Mum isn't there at bedtime. Arun points out that he was hoping for some time soon with Dad to help him learn more about web design. Leila says she would be happy to contribute some recent birthday money from her grandparents and Arun agrees that he would be happy to do this too. Arun suggests that they could clear the attic and do a garage-sale, which would probably raise at least enough for the cable TV subscription and they could have some fun doing it. This prompts Dad to remember that he has been meaning to sell an old record collection. Mum says that she and Dad had been discussing the two living room sofas. Both are rather worn and shabby and she had suggested taking out a loan to buy new ones. She now thinks that perhaps the sofas could hold up for another year or two and instead they could use a loan for a second computer. Arun suggests that some of the other items could be obtained second hand or reconditioned. Leila suggests they make a priority list and that they should talk about how each of them might feel about allowing other family members to use items in their own rooms.

Whether the family ends up with all of the proposed items

or none of them or something completely different is not the issue. There is no fixed outcome, except that it should be mutually agreed. Whether the family budget is enormous or extremely modest, the key is resourcefulness and not deciding beforehand that something must be done in a certain way or that something else is simply not worth considering.

Being creative with time is as important as being creative with money. All too often, adults set up time constraints without sufficiently thinking through the implications for children or considering alternatives that might be required. Many families need at least one adult to work for a family income. Most families will, at some point, need to make appointments with doctors, lawyers, and plumbers. Many families will schedule classes or driving lessons or plane flights. It is not that these things don't matter, but that they do not matter more than our children. They are areas in which we can reach mutual solutions. Can we rearrange work commitments, either in terms of time or venue, to fit in better with family preference? Can we build in flexibility with certain kinds of appointments? Can we arrange alternative care or activities for our children so that they are not committed to unnecessary journeys?

Pam has an early morning doctor's appointment. She has made the appointment at a difficult time knowing that her five-year-old daughter, Elisabeth, likes to wake up slowly and enjoy a leisurely breakfast while watching a favorite cartoon. Pam's partner Alan can often start work at a flexible time, but has an important client to meet on this day. The doctor Pam prefers to see works part-time and her appointments tend to get booked up well in advance. Pam is very concerned about a particular health issue and does not feel that it would be a good idea to wait much longer. The conventional answer would be to take Elisabeth along whatever her protests and to argue that her distress is nothing in comparison to her mother's current anxiety and needs. Some parents would even claim that if Elisabeth objects, it is she who is exerting force and not Pam. Compulsion requires power. Children do not have power over their parents, whereas parents have an automatic power that is easily abused and widely supported. Of course, this one instance of compulsion may do no damage to Elisabeth, but we can't know that with confidence.

So what can Pam do? She could ask the elderly lady over the road, who loves spending time with Elisabeth, to come in and stay with her for an hour. She could explain to Alan that this appointment is very important to her, so important that it might be worth him considering changing his appointment with clients. She could reconsider whether one of the other practice doctors who are more available might not be just as sympathetic and helpful, and rearrange to mid-day when Elisabeth is happy to come along, or to evening when Alan is back home. She could talk to Elisabeth about making the trip to the doctor's a special and fun event. Perhaps Elisabeth could sleep in a comfy tracksuit the night before and be tucked into the car with a blanket and warm drink for the journey. They could take a favorite snack to the waiting room and a favorite picture book, or borrow Alan's hand-held game-boy or his portable cassette player with headphones and story tapes. They could go out for a special breakfast after the appointment or have a breakfast of popcorn at the nearby cinema while seeing a cartoon movie that Elisabeth has expressed interest in.

When we begin from a fixed point with fixed preferences, we are unlikely to succeed in finding consent. Instead, we will end up with either compulsion or self surrender. When we are willing to let go of the idea of inevitable and unchangeable outcomes, we free up the resourcefulness to find mutual solutions. It might be that the solution will contain one or more of the initial starting points. Pam might keep her appointment without any compulsion, for example. The point is simply that real mutual solutions are found when no one is insisting that there can be only one possible outcome, even in situations where resources of money or time are concerned.

Dealing with Emergencies

There are, of course, emergencies: the speeding truck or the meningitis bacteria are no respecters of a parent's wish to reach a mutual solution with his child. When Zoë heard her mother saying, 'we have to go to the hospital right now because Jacob is extremely sick' her preference to keep playing her game and not go anywhere was put aside with ease. Similarly when Barbara snatches her four-year-old daughter Melanie out of the path of a forty-ton lorry it is highly unlikely that Melanie is going to protest that she wasn't consulted first. Barbara will know quite well that her daughter is not suicidal and her aim was not death, but to reach something or someone across the road. Melanie might have a brief moment of shock or distress, but this will quickly evaporate when she sees that her mother is simply helping her to achieve the same end rather more safely.

When Jonathan and Joel arrive at the hospital with their three-year-old son Michael running a high temperature and covered in blotches they would probably be wrong to decide that Michael's delirious screams of 'no' when the doctor approaches are indications that he would rather die than be examined by a stranger, suffer a lumber puncture to test for meningitis or be fitted with a drip to administer antibiotics. Michael almost certainly wants to live, but he is not likely to enjoy pain or fear. Jonathan and Joel should do everything they can to ensure that the doctor respects Michael's wish to be put at ease, to be given treatment in the way most likely to reduce pain within the constraints of the situation, to ameliorate the awful situation whilst also bearing in mind that most of all Michael wants to be well again.

Consent, however, is a much bigger concept than the moment of emergency; as we can see from the examples above consent might not be about the one moment when the emergency is taking place. Barbara knows Melanie well; she is on her side and wants to help her meet her preferences and Barbara knows that in the face of the oncoming truck consent doesn't only refer to that one critical moment, but to life itself. Jonathan and Joel know the same with regard to Michael.

Unfortunately, however, parents have a tendency to overstate emergencies. We can't argue with a truck or a killer virus already active in a child's body, but the same is not true when it comes to a routine inoculation or a dental procedure or stitching up a cut knee. In these cases children are often expected to simply undergo pain, not because it is inevitable or because time is against us in a life and death issue, but simply because it makes a procedure quicker or cheaper or more convenient to the adults involved. No wonder children have trouble distinguishing true emergencies when so many avoidable instances of compulsion are routinely foisted on them as though they were inevitable. Matters of life and death are rare; a family with four children aged nine to sixteen could easily have only ever encountered one such emergency, perhaps a near miss with a car when their youngest was three. Yet parents' minds often immediately jump to such emergencies when they consider letting go of compulsion in their children's lives, as though not to do so would be taking an enormous risk.

Avoiding the Payback

Another way in which the emergency scenario becomes contorted and over-used is in situations where parents think that an action will eventually result in long-term damage to their children. Many cases of compulsion involve the meme that 'enjoyment today will jeopardize long-term well-being.' Regular tooth brushing and diet often come into this category. Parents believe that compulsion now will save pain later, but does this actually justify compulsion?

As we saw previously when discussing consequences, very often even so called natural consequences can be avoided with a bit of thought and assistance. In the folk story of *How the butterfly dies*, a guru gives a child a cocoon and tells him that a butterfly will emerge and that he shouldn't help it. The child does try to help the butterfly to struggle free and it dies instantly. The butterfly's death is put down to the boy's disobedience, but it could equally be put down to the guru's deliberate withholding of essential information. The death was not a natural consequence of rule breaking so much as an outcome of not knowing all of the facts. If some action will result in a long-term ill effect on a child's life then it ought to be possible to set out the information in a way that will convince a child who is used to reasoned argument and consent seeking.

Lamar is ten and has childhood leukemia. The course of treatment has a very good prognosis, but it is debilitating and sometimes very painful. Without the treatment Lamar's prognosis is very poor. Lamar's single parent father, Jordan, has always tried to live by consent with Lamar and to present information fully, without scare mongering or exaggerating. Jordan acknowledges his own limitations and proceeds tentatively. Lamar wants to live. Lamar doesn't want pain, but he knows that he can work with the doctors to limit that pain of the treatment. He doesn't want to give up playing football, but he appreciates that in this instance his preferences have to be part of bigger decisions than the normal daily decisions he has been used to making. Lamar goes ahead with the treatment and makes a full recovery.

In fact very few children, even those not used to living by consent, would refuse treatment in this instance, but the repost from many parents comes in the form of 'but what about those times when not doing x won't result in immediate or medium term death, but will, I'm sure, involve horrible consequences at some point?' The list of things that come into this category is enormous, though getting two parents to actually agree on any definitive 'horror list' would be almost impossible, which should at least alert us to the fact that this horror list may not be as objective and factual as parents claim. The list might include:

- *If my three year old eats sweets she will eventually have to cope with poor dental health and/or health problems from the poisonous additives that these things contain.*
- *If my eleven-year-old son avoids all exercise now he will be at risk later from heart disease and suffer a poorer quality of life.*
- *If my fourteen-year-old daughter doesn't apply herself to academic studies now her options for the future will be stunted and her life will be ruined.*
- *If my five year old refuses medicine for a minor ailment something more serious and long term will happen.*

The list of examples is endless, but the argument for compulsion goes something like this: X activity will result in some cumulative or eventual bad effect. My child only thinks about immediate gratification and can't think in the long term. If I don't use compulsion now it will be too late when the effects start to show, so compulsion is the lesser evil and my child will thank me later.

The argument is false. Firstly, there is that cumulative or eventual bad effect to consider. If we're talking about death from an oncoming truck or diabetic coma or untreated childhood leukemia then children seem very well able to understand the theory of cause and effect. Children do have a grasp of consequences at such times, so, on those occasions when they can't seem to understand it, one of two things might be happening. Firstly, the child might quite reasonably doubt the link that you fear. Secondly, the child might be questioning whether the link is the worst thing that could happen to him.

So let's examine some of these links. Sweets and dental decay don't invariably go together; there are other factors like family history or dental hygiene that make this a remarkably variable picture. Not all sedentary people suffer from heart disease; this is just one possible factor for any given individual. Not everyone who leaves school without qualifications goes on to a dead end life or never takes up adult learning opportunities and not everyone who does get qualifications lives a life of happy fulfillment. A five-year-old refusing medicine might very well recover anyway, perhaps slightly more slowly, but with a stronger immune system in some instances, or perhaps the solution may simply be to find a different way to take medicine that makes it acceptable to the five year old. Parents have a knack for exaggerating the effects of children not doing as they want them to; if the reasons hold up, as they did in Lamar's case, then a reasonable child should be able to assess them and reach a decision.

Even if you can show your child a link between doing x and suffering y, it is still possible for a child to reasonably choose the activity. A statistical link is only that and our children are unique individuals. Moreover the activity may give so much enjoyment that not to choose it would be the irrational option for that particular individual. We all make decisions on the balance of probability, taking into account both statistics about possible risks and our own personal contexts and preferences. A child doing so should not be treated as irrational and incapable of any forward thinking when adults do this all the time as a matter of course. Many sports, for example, have risks attached, but the people who engage in them don't just look at raw statistics, they look at how much they enjoy the sport, what they can do to maximize the thrill whilst minimizing the danger. Sometimes they might even decide that very high risks are worthwhile, not because they are irrational imbeciles, but because this is what matters to an individual most. Children do the same; having the perfect functioning body along with the perfect test scores might actually be so mind-numbingly boring and miserable to a particular child that her life is hardly worth living. Can this really be for her own good?

Using compulsion because we think we are acting in our children's best interests is a losing strategy (as I discussed in Chapter 6). Firstly, we could be wrong; our assumptions, even our most dearly held best ideas are not infallible. Secondly, compulsion causes distress that risks damaging another person's ability to think clearly; if we think our children are not thinking reasonably about a situation it is rather improbable that we will improve the situation by adding in more distress and muddled thinking. Thirdly, we are simply not the child; we have an incredibly important role in our children's lives, but we can't inhabit their minds, we can't be them and ultimately we can't live their lives for them. We do our children a much greater service by giving lots of information than by taking away their self-determination.

None of us want our children to suffer, now or in the future, but when our urge to protect and help our offspring becomes one of the things causing present suffering then something is deeply wrong with our parenting logic.

- Compulsion now is pain now and using pain now to prevent pain later hardly adds up to reasonable thinking.
- If an action now will have genuine long-term effects then this ought to be explicable to a reasonable child used to living by consent.
- Many long-term effects are based on the best guess we have with available information. We may be convinced, but we should not exaggerate the information.
- Decisions about preferences are likely to take into account much more than long term effects; this is only one factor and we can't decide that it is the only or the paramount factor on another's behalf.

Safety First

Compulsion on safety grounds isn't always about possible future consequences. There is a conventional consensus that in matters of present safety, parents know best and should over-ride their children's decisions. There are times when there is a genuine matter of life and death at stake and parents do have to make fast decisions and talk later, but, as we have seen these are rare exceptions. In normal situations, however, I want to suggest that such thinking puts children in more, not less, danger.

Whether our children are trying to decide what they'd like to eat for dinner or facing difficult decisions about smoking, drugs, extreme sports or what career to explore they are still the same unique people being assisted to reach a solution that does not go against their particular self. We, as parents, have a lot to offer; information, moral views, assumptions and experience, but none of this is infallible. Parents who defend compulsion as a way of preparing their children for the real world are mistaken on the issue of safety as on any other. In the real world being someone who seeks advice from parents or other trusted adults and who has a resourceful, reasonable, flexible, open-minded problem-solving approach to life is not only an excellent way to live now, but also the best preparation for the future.

Childcare experts sometimes propose that giving our children 'firm boundaries' is a way of giving them the security they need and crave. It is true that such artificial boundaries can give a sense of safety, but they often do so at a high cost. Along with the protection may come a hunger for a lifetime of security and certainty, an unwillingness to ask too many uncomfortable questions, and a dangerous willingness to obey without question. Fostering internal security and confidence through consent seeking, on the other hand, is a much more worthwhile process. To have a child who is able to find solutions, listen to and weigh criticism, assess advice before making decisions and take responsibility for her decisions is eminently safer.

- Life and death safety decisions are rare; most of the time we do have other choices.
- Compulsion only protects children in a short term and negative fashion.
- Living by consent fosters the growth of internal safety mechanisms such as advice seeking, reasoned assessment of risks and benefits, flexibility and openness.
- Safety ultimately owes more to internal attitudes than to external boundaries.

Solutions Are Out There

The best preparation for life is resourcefulness and problem solving. One very pervasive and very bad meme that gets in the way of consent based parenting is the notion that some problems are simply insoluble. When we stop believing this and realize that solutions are out there, even on those occasions when our human limitations get in the way of us finding them, then we tend to have a more positive, creative approach not only to parenting, but to life.

The question is, do we actually believe that the real world is one in which solutions exist (at least theoretically)? If our perception of the universe is pessimistic or we think some things are simply inevitable, then solutions will remain very hard to find. If we are optimistic that there are solutions, even when we don't always find them, then we will go on improving.

Let's consider the Gates family and their three children. Mum has heard about consensual living and thinks it might be for them, but she has lots of questions. Dad thinks it's a mad idea. Liberty (18) thinks it might work for older teenagers, but surely the younger ones need compulsion to keep them in line? Dinah (14) and Peter (13) think it sounds great, but they're skeptical too; they think Mum will resort to compulsion when the chips are down.

Today is a busy day. Dad has a pile of work he wants to get through. Liberty is leaving for an important holiday with friends and wants a lift to the airport. Dinah really wants to see a certain friend today, who lives some distance away from the city in an area not served by public transport. Liberty and Dinah have already had a row. Liberty thinks Dinah's trip is unimportant as she could see her friend any time and wants Mum to take her to the airport instead of taking Dinah to the friend's house. Dinah thinks Liberty always gets everything her way. Dinah hasn't seen her friend in ages and there is a bus straight to the airport. Peter wants to go to a park today, as he's been practicing some new stunts on his skateboard and wants to try some more. He also wants pizza for lunch. Mum wants to get through the day sane and hopes for a cup of coffee (with caffeine!) at some point. Dad says it's nothing to do with him, he has to earn a living and, by the way, 'Didn't I tell you that you couldn't all get what you want.'

The best scenarios are going to occur when everyone in the family subscribes to finding mutual solutions and seeking consent, but even here there are possible solutions. We have to remember that solutions ultimately have to be the ones that particular people prefer. Knowing that a solution is theoretically possible doesn't always give us the resourcefulness to find it, but it does make us look at things differently. It is an enormous mind shift that has a real effect. We also have to remember that the final solution may not look anything like the initial problems. The art of finding mutual solutions is the art of resourcefulness and openness. We can change our preferences; something better can come along at any moment.

Any number of things could happen. Dad might be persuaded to take just a long enough break to take Liberty to the airport, freeing up Mum to drive with Dinah and Peter to Dinah's friend's, pick up the friend, and take them all to a pizza restaurant near a park. The girls could have time together and Peter could skateboard. Mum could get two cappuccinos at the restaurant and read half a novel in the park.

Dad might be totally intransigent and remain outside of the loop. Mum, however, might remember that there is a new movie opening today that Dinah and Peter both want to see. She could drop them at the cinema on the way to the airport. Before setting out, she could ring the mother of Dinah's friend, who might agree to bring her daughter for an overnight stay later that day. Then, after the friend arrives, Mum and Peter could head for the park via McDonalds (Peter having changed his preference about what he wants to eat) and Mum could relax in the park café with delicious coffee and cakes. Alternatively, Dad may remain fixed, but Mum finds that Dinah and Peter would rather go bowling than go to a friend's or to the park, so she drops them on the way to taking Liberty to the airport and joins them there later for her coffee.

It might be that Dad stops being a grump and realizes that he has a client he could visit who lives close by Dinah's friend. He could take her without interrupting his work and today he'd prefer the client trip to the office. Mum will take Liberty to the airport, then have an afternoon to herself in the city. Peter is now happy to stay home; with Dad out of the office he can have access to the computer. Or something else entirely different could happen.

The point is that there is not some fixed, pre-determined solution out there that has to be mystically divined, nor is it that there are no solutions and someone has to suffer. Rather, we can build consensual 'win-win' families if we start by believing that solutions are always theoretically possible. Solutions are as practical and available as our own resourcefulness. What prevents us finding solutions is not that they don't exist, but that we are limited.

Owning and recognizing our limitations does not mean that we have to get stuck on it. We make mistakes. These mistakes need not lead us to despair, but can be used as opportunities for learning and growth. Conventional wisdom tells us that mistakes are bad and that guilt will follow. Conventional parenting seems to have two main responses to parental mistakes. The first is to wallow in guilt, feeling that we can never get it right, endlessly agonizing and mentally beating ourselves up for not being able to do it all, be it all, and give up anything we ever wanted with a smile. The second is to claim that we can only do what we can do, that we can only be 'good enough' and that children have to learn to lose sometimes.

If we choose to live by consent then we won't have to take either of these paths. We will still make mistakes because we can only act from the best ideas we have at any one time and we do get tired or find some things hard to think clearly about. When this happens we don't need to fall into paroxysms of guilt and neither do we need to think that a mistake means we can never find a solution in a similar situation. We can always apologize when we make mistakes and we can also use the situation to learn from. Being able to say that we were wrong and then move on to develop new ideas should be the cause of celebration, not guilt.

Sometimes, of course, we don't understand why we make particular mistakes. We may have all sorts of triggers hidden deep within our psyche or which arise from ideas that we have taken in without ever being able to articulate them. We may never fully get to the bottom of some inexplicit assumptions, but we can at least learn to notice our triggers. We can spend time thinking about ways to disengage or behave differently when those triggers arise. We always have a choice.

When we see our own mistakes as things that we can change and learn from, we also start to treat our children's mistakes differently. Children are limited, too. Conventional parenting often assumes that children do certain things to test their parents, or to deliberately engage in a power struggle over rightful parental boundaries. Children are not the enemy; they are simply limited like us.

One great resource in finding solutions is to question everything: Why should we all go to sleep at 11p.m. and get up at 7.30 a.m.? Why should parents (or anyone) be seen as figures of authority? Why do we believe that compulsion can be justified for some perceived benefit like clean teeth? Why shouldn't our children stay in their pajamas all day? Why do we think the world will end if our children drink coke or love watching TV? The list is endless. When we start to seek consent then life is not about conventional wisdom, but about real individuals with real preferences and real problems to solve. It is a process in which our whole worldview is likely to constantly change. It is both enormously scary and endlessly liberating.

- Believe that everyone can win; if you don't really think that a solution exists you won't be committed to looking for it.
- Accept that you will make mistakes and so will your children, but don't wallow in guilt or give up; learn from mistakes.
- The best living comes when we question everything.

11
Winning is for Parents

For many, the pendulum has already swung too far and there is a fear abroad of greedy, needy children who will suck their parents dry before asking for more. So why seek consent with children? Why not lay down the boundaries and try to redress the balance before it's too late? The fact is that the greedy, needy child is not a child who is getting what she wants.

It can't be stressed too much; self interest is not immoral and children are not born wicked with desires that only cause harm for themselves and others. Sadly, we come to believe these things through a process of making subjective observations of children who are, for much of the time, thwarted and treated as unreasonable beings. This simply results in vicious cycles of self-fulfilling prophecy. If children and adults are seen as opposing forces competing for scarce resources then this is what we will experience, but it doesn't have to be that way.

Self interest does not have to be opposed to doing the right thing. There is no reason why the motivation of reasonable, creative, trustworthy people (also known as children) should tend to be bad. Once children experience operating within a win-win environment they have no reason to think in oppositional terms; helping others in their family to get their needs met is no longer a matter of competition or turn taking.

Neither is this lifestyle merely about material consumption. Finding mutual solutions is not a knee jerk response involving the instant provision of every whim. It is a real and genuine process of finding solutions that work for all involved in the particular context of real families, whether we are millionaires or scraping by. Finding mutual solutions is ultimately much less exhausting and much more fulfilling than fighting with our children. Moreover consent seeking parenting is better for us too.

- A child getting what she wants is not about parents losing.
- We need to forget the oppositional view of parents versus children in favor of building a win-win home.
- Living by consent is good for children, but it is also good for us; if self interest and altruism can co-exist in children, then the same is true for parents.
- Consent based parenting is also self interested, self-fulfilling parenting.

The Self Fulfilling Parent

The first question most parents ask when faced with any parenting technique is, 'Does it work?' I want to suggest that this is the wrong starting point. Consent-based parenting is a way of life that answers the question, 'What is the best way to relate to my children?' This starting point helps us to keep trying again and to go on learning how to find solutions despite our own limitations. Consent based parenting is not easy or magical; it takes work, involves a lot of effort in overcoming bad ideas, will include moments of failure and often seems counter cultural. If we are going to embark on consent based parenting we therefore need to be convinced that we are doing the best and the right thing. I am certainly convinced. Why?

Firstly, there is nothing inherent in the nature of children that makes them less human than any other person. Children are fully human and it is a feature of human beings that they are unique individuals worthy of equal respect and serious consideration. Too much conventional parenting practice ignores this basic humanity, just as racism or sexism ignores the full humanity of anyone who is not white and male. Children lack experience and have a particular dependency on adults in terms of survival needs, but this dependency is not the logical opposite of basic humanity and selfhood.

Secondly, we have unique obligations towards the children we give birth to or choose to parent by adoption and, though no obligation can be infinite, the special obligation of parents to children is considerable and far reaching. This in itself is a very good reason to find the best possible way of relating to our children.

Thirdly, our position as trusted moral advisors with unique obligations towards our children is completely undermined if we do not behave in the best way towards our children. In other words, we cannot expect children to treat our advice and moral ideas with any serious or reasoned consideration if we are treating them badly whilst we dole out moral advice.

So often, for example, young people are given advice about drugs in the form of a simple 'don't go there' by parents who regularly drink alcohol and perhaps smoke. Not only can their children see that double standards are operating (arguments of illegality aside) but they might also feel that people who routinely treated them unjustly and manipulatively are not people they want to learn morality from. None of us are paragons of absolute virtue and our children are quite able to appreciate that; we don't have to have arrived at sainthood before we can share our moral ideas, but we should at least be honest about being on our own learning journeys and not simply presume that adulthood confers the power to use compulsion against children whilst we tell them how to live.

Duncan and Lindsay are two sixteen year olds who are embarking on a sexual relationship. Duncan's parents have shared lots of information with him about respecting his own and other people's autonomy, and have also given him lots of practical and health related advice. Lindsay's parents, on the other hand, have not only had a catalogue of disastrous relationships themselves, but are adamant that they will do all in their power to stop Lindsay and Duncan from getting together. In the latest bruising encounter, Lindsay's mother screamed a string of abusive terms at her before grounding her for a weekend. Why would Lindsay want to listen to 'advice' on relationships from someone who not only has made little attempt to nurture good relationships in her own life, but also treats her with utter disrespect, preferring name calling and the issuing of commands to information and reason?

- We have a particular moral obligation towards our children.
- It is simply wrong to assume that we can take away someone else's autonomy, even on the basis that the other person is a child.
- None of us are perfect or have all the answers to life, but our moral advice to our children will be treated with much more respect and consideration if we are not behaving hypocritically; doling out morality on the one hand whilst compelling our children on the other.
- Consent based parenting allows us to relate to our children better than any other form of parenting; this is good for them, but it's good for us too.

The Involved Parent

Spending a lot of time with someone who we are in constant conflict with is emotionally and physically exhausting. When we replace conflict and competition with problem solving and resourcefulness, the parent-child relationship is not a chore, but a joy. Consent based parenting is not an instant panacea, but it is the most rewarding parenting I have ever encountered, for myself as much as anyone else in my family.

Do you remember Hayley and her Mum, Kate? A couple of years after deciding to live by consent, Kate has redesigned her working life. She loves the design side of her interior decorating business, but has delegated more of the management and customer relations tasks. The shared clothes-making project for Hayley's twelfth birthday, which first inspired the family to begin making changes in their lifestyle and investigating consent based living, sparked a shared interest in design and crafts. At fourteen, Hayley is designing and making her own clothes, has a strong interest in beadwork and is learning silversmith from a craftswoman Kate met through work. With more time on her hands, Kate and Hayley have also discovered a shared passion for movies and enjoy one another's company. Money in this household is not tight, but it is not quite so readily available as when Kate was working seventy-hour weeks and saving on management salaries for her business, especially since Ramesh, Hayley's Dad, decided that he also wanted to make some changes. Ramesh gave up his job in a large public relations company eighteen months ago to concentrate on setting up his own small company. He still works relatively long hours and for slightly less money, but his office is home based and he has more flexibility. Ramesh also discovered that when he stopped merely buying things for Hayley and expecting her never to inconvenience him with her actual presence, that his daughter was an interesting person who he could share some of his fitness activities with.

Decision making in the household has become a very different activity than it was two years ago. Ramesh and Kate don't feed Hayley an endless stream of expensive gifts while ignoring her opinions and accusing her of being ungrateful and sullen. Hayley doesn't constantly want to spend more and more only to get instantly bored and feel permanently dissatisfied. When an activity is being decided on or a purchase is being considered there isn't a rush to simply appease Hayley in the hope that she will go away and leave the adults to get on with their lives. Instead the family are actually living together, making decisions together, questioning preferences and coming up with something better or going back to the original preference if it seems like the best idea after all. In short, Ramesh and Kate are involved with their daughter's life and she has much more trust in and liking for her parents.

So often parents and children do not like each other's company and this is hardly surprising when the whole ethos of the house is one of confrontation and competition. It is hard, when we are trapped in cycles of compulsion and trying to assert control over children, to imagine that it could actually be very pleasant to engage more fully with our children. When we see children as sullen, moody, expensive or hard to motivate then we are not likely to want to be even more involved with them. Living by consent breaks into this cycle; by putting everyone on the same side, engagement becomes not a chore, but an increasingly easy and fulfilling part of parenting. This doesn't mean that parents and children have to become joined at the hip. Sometimes being involved simply means helping children to set up activities that we are not part of or giving one another space for individual development and growth. It does mean, however, that parents and children aren't reluctant to be in one another's company or to help one another meet their preferences.

- Engaging constructively with our children is a demanding feature of parenting, but it is not emotionally exhausting and conflict laden in the way that trying to control children is.
- Involvement is not about living one another's lives or never having any personal time or space, but it does allow for joint projects between family members and for a flow of valued input into one another's lives.
- Consent seeking parents, and not just their children, benefit from having positive and creative family relationships in their lives

The Winning Parent

Let me stress the point again, being an engaged parent is a benefit of consent based parenting and it does not entail giving up your own life. Sucked-dry parents are not parents who are finding consent with their children. Consent-based parenting is parenting in which everyone wins; even you, the parent. Self surrender does sometimes occur, but it is not a good thing and we need to be able to recognize it and move away from it to genuine consent based living. We are all limited and self surrender happens because sometimes:

- we lack resourcefulness on some issues.
- we are too tired or stressed to think of a good solution.
- we have set up a situation badly resulting in that 'locked in' feeling.
- we are dealing with an area where we are prey to bad ideas.
- we lack practice at and/or belief in mutual solutions

Self surrender is easy to spot because we are likely to react badly to our situation and to our children when we are chronically locked into it. We know we are simply giving in when:

- we never or seldom prefer the solution to any given problem-solving attempt.
- we think that it's inevitable that parents should sacrifice themselves to their children no matter how bad we feel.
- we notice that we are volatile; guilt ridden one minute, resentful and angry the next.
- we observe children who are more and more demanding and expect their first preference to be met without question.

- we feel less and less creative when faced with everyday problems.

We live in a society that tells us both that children are boundary-pushing ogres who must be restricted if you we are to survive and that parents should expect a life of self surrender in return for having children. These contradictory and damaging ideas need challenging; living by consent offers family relationships that include adult fulfillment without child neglect and without having to make our own children into the enemy. Parental self surrender is bad for everyone, including children, as it:

- robs children of good models of problem solving.
- short circuits children's resourcefulness and ability to develop new ideas.
- gives children the idea that childhood is a time of self gratification whilst adulthood is about a life of drudgery.
- maintains the idea that someone has to lose.
- builds up parental resentment, which children will ultimately suffer from.

Self surrender is also bad for us and we don't need it in our life. Unless we really enjoy being whining martyrs who want to hand on warped and limited views of adult life and problem solving to our children then we need to work at ridding ourselves of it. The cycle of wanting to avoid compulsion, but not having the resourcefulness and problem solving mechanisms to do so, and ending up either losing ourselves or forcing our child to lose is unhealthy for everyone. Parents too are supposed to benefit from consent-based parenting. We can only begin to break this cycle when we convince ourselves that life doesn't have to be like this; self surrender is not noble and good; it's exhausting and bad. So how do we resist it?

- Believe that solutions exist. If we think finding solutions is like a mythical quest for the Holy Grail then we may as well give up now and get used to a life of someone having to lose.
- If we are convinced that solutions exist then we will never be satisfied with self surrender. Instead, even when it happens we will be ready to learn and move on.
- Practice being creative; it's like a muscle, the more experiences of mutual problem solving we have the easier it gets.
- Respect every family member; parents included. Our children can only take our wishes and ideas into account if we are clear about them and if our wishes are communicated without the manipulative overtones of martyrdom or thinly veiled threats.

- This means that we have to give some thought to what we want in our lives. Of course we should be prepared to change our minds, but it is worth starting from knowing what our mind is.

Let's take Nuala and Donal McManus and their children Ardal (13) and Finn (11). Nuala is a seasoned martyr. The family can guarantee that when consulted about what to do for a family day out or where to go to eat or where to take holidays, Nuala will always utter a variation of, 'I don't mind, I'll do whatever you boys want.' They also know that in fact Nuala does mind and that if they 'guess' the wrong place or restaurant or holiday destination, Nuala will communicate her misery in a million underhand ways whilst insisting that 'nothing is wrong' and that she 'doesn't mind' and that no-one should worry about her.

The strain on the McManus family is enormous. Despite everyone's rather polished skills in second guessing Nuala's real wishes, many days are wasted in everyone feeling ill at ease or down right miserable. Nuala is miserable, yet she is also the most dominant person in the family. She would of course tell you otherwise, but how can she not be when so much energy is going into meeting her hidden needs while the others try to mold their own preferences around a guessing game that can't be won. Nuala insists that with four competing lots of preferences to take into account, someone has to lose and it is best if it is her, but her idea that this is the best way to live is clearly not born out in the stress and anxiety her family have about almost everything they do. Nuala is wrong; this is neither the best nor the only way to live and in fact not only is she losing, but everyone is losing. Moreover this lose/win environment is very unstable and hurtful.

Nuala also insists that she behaves this way because she loves her husband and children so much, but what she is giving them is not love at all; what she is doing is lazy and manipulative. Nuala is withholding her resourcefulness, and running her family ragged in pointless mind games instead of helping them to grow as reasoning, flexible people with their inner motivation in tact. This is very far from loving no matter what Nuala intends by it.

Nuala's martyr complex is actually full of fear; she mistrusts her own abilities to find solutions, she is frightened that if she puts her needs and preferences into the pot she will lose and she will suffer rejection and failure. She is so afraid of not finding success and happiness that she deliberately lives in a way that will never allow her to find out if life could have been better. Although Nuala thinks of her stance as an enormous gift, allowing the other three to get their way more often without her preferences complicating things further what is actually taking place is a trade war in which

Nuala's chronic and entrenched self-sacrifice is a loan demanding returns with interest and menaces. One of those menaces is that self surrender is held up as the icon of good family interaction; if Mum is so willing to put herself last then the least everyone else can do is return the favor and put themselves last; they should be willing to guess what their all-giving Mum would really like and forget that they ever had preferences in the first place. Ultimately, everyone loses and everyone sacrifices in this household.

Nuala may seem like a rather extreme example, but most of us have met and recognize some version of her; perhaps in one of our own parents, perhaps, at least in part, in some of our own parenting ideas or practices. Pretending that we can eradicate ourselves from the picture when it comes to parenting always fails; miserable parents communicate misery to their children and give their children bleak outlooks on adult life. We owe it to ourselves and to our children to consider ourselves, value our own preferences, think about how they can be met and act as though solutions exist. We don't have to compel or become a selfish neglectful monster; anymore than a child getting what she wants has to become a greedy sociopath. If Nuala could let go of her chronic martyr complex what might the McManus family look like?

The family has just been through a rough patch. Donal has been ill and time away from work strained the family finances. Now things are getting back to normal and, in the meantime, Donal and Nuala have been thinking a lot about their parenting and about the benefits of non-compulsion and consent. Nuala finds the new way of thinking challenging to say the least, but Ardal and Finn are very good at reminding her that they only want to hear from her if she can state her preferences or offer alternative ideas to other people. It's Friday evening; Donal is feeling much better and the family decides that they need some fun.

Donal suggests that he and Nuala should go for a meal while leaving the boys (now aged 14 and 12) with a take away and some rented videos. Nuala wants to see a particular movie that has just been released and says so straight out. Finn is happy to stay home with the videos and a take away pizza, but Ardal wants to get out of the house and doesn't feel like being left with responsibility as the oldest brother. He's also quite keen to see a movie, though he's not sure which one and is fairly certain he won't share his Mum's taste in movies. Donal is happy to help the boys do something other than stay at home, but he particularly wants to be able to spend some time alone with Nuala and its seems to him a long time since they last went out alone together.

They spend a long time tossing around ideas until they find a mutual solution. In the end, Finn phones his friend Declan and arranges to stay at his house overnight; on the way to dropping Finn off the family collect pizza and some videos for him and Declan. Nuala, Donal and Ardal go to a multiplex cinema with a nearby selection of cafés and restaurants. Ardal's film starts half an hour later than the one Naula and Donal are seeing so he takes some money to buy a burger before his film. Naula and Donal are out of their movie earlier than Ardal, giving them time to have a drink and snack in a tapas bar with some time to themselves.

- Self surrender is hard work. Finding solutions can be demanding too, but while the former leads to misery and everyone losing, the latter leads to resourcefulness and fulfillment for everyone concerned.
- Self surrender is bad for us and our children; we all deserve better.

The Changing Parent

When we replace compulsion with consent, the life of everyone in the family changes with exciting consequences, but building consent into out lives is not simply a matter of avoiding compulsion; it is much more positive than this. It is about replacing vicious cycles with new relationships in which respect, resourcefulness, reasonableness, new ideas and individual preferences figure largely.

This benefits everyone. We live in a society where children are routinely deprived of the common rights of humanity, where they often cannot choose what to eat or wear, whom they associate with, when they can sleep, what they can learn or even what they can enjoy as leisure. Love is neither compensation nor justification for such a total lack of basic control and the distress that results is not character building or a preparation for living in the real world. It simply damages children's ability to problem solve creatively and reasonably. It perpetuates an acceptance of suffering and an inability to follow one's preferences into adulthood. Children who are used to consent do not expect to never have to solve problems nor do they think that life will be handed to them on a plate, but they are optimistic that solutions exist. We live in a society that sees parenthood as burdensome, but with consent this too can change.

Let's take the Gregory family. Anita has been at home with the children, who are educated at home, for several years. She generally likes to be home-based, but wants more activities which will stretch her mind and skills. She also dislikes the house they've lived in for the last five years. Leroy works for a children's charity. His work is stressful, often demands that he puts in extra hours and is low paid. Leroy has wanted a change for some time, but he feels stuck. Opportunities in his specialist area are few enough but he really feels that he would like a complete change, though he is not sure what to. Leroy worries a lot about money; the family has debts, which are manageable, but Leroy hardly feels that he should be rocking the boat. They have three children, Carmel (15), Enrique (14) and Marina (10). The family has worked hard on finding consensual solutions for the last four years and this has improved their family life enormously, but the adults still have a tendency to believe that certain things are fixed in stone, especially when it comes to the conditions of their own lives.

Anita puts a lot of thought into this and decides to start thinking about what she would really like her life to be like. She wants an activity that is hers, preferably with some money attached and she would particularly like to explore her writing talents; she wants to move house, preferably out of the city to somewhere where the children could each have their own room without Carmel and Marina having to share; she wants to get out of debt; she wants to see more of Leroy. After a while Anita shares her wish list with Leroy and opens conversations with Leroy and the children about how they could make big changes. Leroy is skeptical about whether they could make such radical changes, but he is increasingly disenchanted with his present work. He would like to do some consultancy work for charities and voluntary sector organizations rather than being tied to one organization, but he is very anxious about money, not only because of debts, but because they are in a situation where, after a period of negative equity on their current house, the house sale would yield only a very tiny deposit for a new house.

When it comes to the children, Carmel is someone who likes her own space and her own company. She would certainly like a room of her own where she could spread out her art materials without them being covered in Marina's toys and clothes. Enrique is active and gregarious. He is quite content with their current house and enjoys the city and seeing lots of friends, but he is also interested in the idea of living somewhere where he could learn to canoe and climb. Marina feels more ambivalent; she likes the idea of her own room, but otherwise feels settled where she is, though she's willing to keep an open mind.

Three years later the family is living in the countryside, in a four bed roomed house. Leroy has set up his consultancy business and it is very slow going, but he is making just enough to form a basic income for the family and he has much more time to spend with them and feels happier. Anita is still spending lots of time helping the children with their education and life, but she is also spending a lot of time writing and beginning to get a few commissions and make a little money. Carmel, now 18, is about to go to college to study for an art degree, having taken some distance learning courses and spent the last six months working intensively on her portfolio apprenticed to a local artist. Enrique, at 17, has lots of new friends, spends time canoeing and abseiling and is starting on a mountain leadership-training course while doing part time work at one of the outdoor pursuits centers in the area. Thirteen-year-old Marina loves the freedom of the countryside much more than she thought she would and with digital TV and her own computer she doesn't feel that she is missing out. She has made new friends in the local village and joined a local drama group.

Consent based parenting is not like one of those annoying Internet adverts that pop up on your screen unbidden proclaiming that, 'Six months ago I was homeless and destitute, now I'm a millionaire – all you have to do is press this button....' Making changes is often slow and demands a lot of resourcefulness, but as we nurture an environment of consent for our children, we tend to start to do the same for ourselves too. Once we start to live as though we can solve the everyday problems like what we all want to eat for tea or when and where everyone will sleep, then we start to live as though we can solve other problems too. We start to live as though individuals matter, even when that individual is our self. Living like this causes changes, many of them subtle and imperceptible until we look back and see how far we've come. We should certainly parent by consent for the sake of our children but we can, without any guilt, do it for ourselves too; we all win.

What's so great about consent-based parenting for the parent?

- It helps us to maximize our own self-interest and motivation.
- It enables us to relate to our children in the best way.
- It puts us in a position to be trusted by our children as sources of advice, information and review.
- It enhances the way we relate to our children and our ability to share projects with them.
- Everyone wins; even parents.
- Energy is diverted from conflict into resourcefulness.
- There is a constant cycle of new ideas. It's not just children who are learning all the time, but parents too.

12
Winning is for Everyone

Not only is consent a winning strategy for parents, but children can and should have their own way. We can parent by consent, not compulsion, and, in the process, meet our children's preferences and our own. Living by consent is just what it says it is; a way of finding mutual solutions. What stand in our way, most of all, is not the practicalities of time or money or resources, which are surmountable, but bad ideas, but we can take control of our ideas. We can question everything and by so doing begin to break vicious cycles in favor of new ways of thinking and relating within families. This is a long process, but having some tools can help us to build the benefits into our families, so I want to summarize some of the ideas that assist us in finding new ways of living by consent and go on to suggest a 'toolkit' of attitudes.

Helping Ourselves to Help Our Children

Remember we might be wrong

'I might be wrong' is a very powerful idea when it comes to parenting. There are, of course, many ideas that we hold and are absolutely certain of in our own mind. We might even actually be right, but we should not lose sight of our basic limitations. Parents should most definitely share their opinions, particularly their moral opinions as fully as possible, but our limitations and the fact that ultimately we are not the person making the decision prevent us from being final arbiters.

Help our children to trust us

Conventional parents often assume that a 'contract' exists between themselves and their children in which they provide food, warmth, shelter, and protection whilst their children owe various levels of duty or obedience in return. Where does this contract come from? In any other sphere of life we agree that both parties of a contract have to knowingly sign up for a contract to be valid. Furthermore we have procedures for circumstances in which contracts may be broken and ended, as in the case of divorce or an early settlement of a bank loan etc. Yet in this case we simply assume a contract by virtue of a child being born and assume that the child, who has never agreed the terms in the first place, has no way out of the contract barring the most extreme cases of abuse. This kind of contract is assumed every time a child is forced to do chores or to take part in some activity, which is deemed to be for the good of the family without any reference to the good of the individual child.

Consent-based parents acknowledge that parental responsibility is not matched by a corresponding duty or obligation. This does not mean that the relationship in practice is one sided or that parents will spend their lives discharging obligations while children simply take and take. We do well to be aware of our basic obligations, but this is never more than a basic starting point. Once children trust that they are not going to be compelled and do not have to compete against their parents they are more than willing to assist their parents in meeting their preferences too. Children can see that consensual solutions make for much better relationships.

Be involved, not forceful

We care enormously for our children and want the best for them at all times. Unfortunately this excellent motive can easily become an excuse for compulsion and for preventing children from getting the best by their own lights. Consent-based parents believe that love is not a good reason to compel someone. That does not mean that we simply throw our hands in the air and let them 'get on with it'. Parents have active, involved, moral roles, but not forceful ones. Love matters, our opinions are important, our criticism is a gift, but none of those are sufficient to over-ride another person.

Go beyond 'I hear what you say'

Many conventional parents believe that they are not acting authoritatively because they spend a good deal of time listening, negotiating or even compromising, but they still cling to some bottom line beyond which they insist the final decision must be theirs. This kind of parenting often involves offering choices, 'You can watch TV for one hour or play on the computer for one hour, but you can't watch TV for as long as you like and then move onto the computer'; 'You can eat ice cream or chocolate or cake, but you are not having that disgusting stuff full of artificial colors.' Choices often mask the reality that a free decision is simply not on offer.

The consent-based parent respects the child's ability to reach a mutual solution. This means that there is no list of pre-approved outcomes to choose from. It doesn't mean that we have to stock one million flavors of ice cream in our freezers or that we have to be able to provide every conceivable activity known to humanity at the drop of a hat, but it does meant that we need to be open minded about what a solution might look like.

Trust our children

We have a lot of ideas that make us fearful of people who act out of self-interest, but in fact self-interest and morality are not logical opposites and a child getting what she want does not have to mean that others will lose out. Children who become accustomed to living within a win-win ethos have no vested interest in seeing anyone else in their family lose. There is no longer an atmosphere of competition, so helping others to meet their preferences is likely to benefit everyone involved.

You don't have to be afraid that children who get what they want will become spoiled and selfish. Generally, children who are labeled 'spoiled' are unhappy children, whose needs may seem to being met on the surface whilst they actually wrestle with a huge hunger that is going totally unidentified and/or unmet. That is not helping children to get what they want by consent-based living. Having a strong sense of self, knowing what you want in life and working to achieve it are not wrong and don't need to be opposed to altruism.

Find mutual solutions

To reach consent we have to stop relying on short-cuts and start using reasonableness and resourcefulness to find mutual solutions that everyone prefers. We don't have to embark on every decision as though we know nothing about the people we're interacting with. We bring to our family decisions a whole set of observations, knowledge about what has helped in the past, shared ways of using language, family culture and so on. What we don't have, though, are fixed blue prints; we might have an excellent guess based on lots of previous knowledge that in situation x, y will probably work well, but we also need to remain open minded and flexible so that we don't fall into the situation of actually deciding ahead that in situation x we must always do y.

Don't be a doormat

The aim is always to achieve mutual consent; not compulsion, not self surrender, but consent. Creating an environment of consent involves thinking ahead, building on win-win situations and maximizing everyone's wishes. It is not merely a negative, compulsion avoidance lifestyle, but a positive, optimistic lifestyle that questions both adult centered power imbalances and ideas that being a parent demands a life of self-negation.

Stay optimistic

So where will it all end up? Unlike conventional parents, consent-based parents do not attempt to prescribe or predict outcomes for their children. Living by consent is about getting the best out of today so that we gradually build up a process for living that is creative, reasoned and moral. We can't describe its ends at the outset. Many people find this rather daunting or even disappointing, but when we think more carefully about this it is not hard to see that the idea that we can test a parenting theory is always false. We are not dealing with mathematical formula. We are not dealing with inert raw materials that can be input into a manufacturing process to ensure a specific product at the other end. We are dealing with people: real, fully human, free, limited people. We might be able to make some general guesses that children who are treated as autonomous human beings will behave as reasoning, flexible, open-minded, truth seeking, innovative individuals, but what the detailed content of that might look like in any given individual is much more open ended. This is actually a very good thing; if you can describe exactly who a free and creative person will be at the age of eighteen then all you have is a cardboard stereotype and not a free person at all. This unpredictability is not something to fear; reasoning, self interested people will make the world a much better place, even if we can't yet describe what that better place might look like.

A Winning Toolkit

Consent based relationships don't have blue prints, but they do involve changing our attitudes and transferring our energies away from compulsion, self surrender, opposing wills and setting artificially decided controls into a way of life that is much more positive. This is a flexible process that involves constantly working on new ideas, but along the way a 'toolkit' of attitudes assists.

Consent

Consent is crucial and is not only about avoiding compulsion. Many of the examples in this book have been about people caught between a rock and a hard place trying to avoid compulsion. Compulsion between parents and children is certainly something that we do well to live without it. When we begin trying to live by consent we may find initially that all we are doing is struggling not to compel, but the most creative ways of living as a family emerge when we move on and begin positively building a new environment of consent.

We need to use the quiet, calm spaces to think about ways of building consent into our lives, ways of avoiding the hard cases arising so that they do so less and less often and eventually hardly at all. We need to have flexible ideas about things that generally work well. How can we use space in our homes to help everyone function optimally? How can we resource our homes to help everyone meet their needs and wishes? We need to have a few 'Disney solutions' up our sleeves (things that we know will help our family avoid impasses) so that we don't get trapped in losing situations.

Reasonableness

Everyone can reason at a level appropriate to their wishes and development. The tiniest baby knows how to get love and warmth and this is as rational as the physicist getting a research grant by delivering a polished presentation. To trust this basic reasonableness requires a great deal of openness and flexibility from all participants. It involves both sharing information and being willing to change our minds and take up new and better ideas.

Recognizing Limitations

If we think we are always right then consent will never get off the ground. An environment of consent has to be one in which no one is perfect or authoritative and no one is dismissed.

Resourcefulness

When we are busy merely avoiding compulsion or trying to find solutions in very hard situations our creativity can feel extremely elusive. At such times it is often better to go for solutions that simply give us some breathing space; do something completely different and think about the problem another time, when it is not immediate or stressful. On the other hand, the more we have experience of win-win situations and the more we build consent into the fabric of our family relationships, the more resourceful we tend to become. Resourcefulness is simply about finding better solutions that work for everyone and we are more likely to find those solutions when we are not stressed or up against the clock so thinking ahead is an excellent way to become more resourceful.

Flexibility

Reason and resourcefulness are assisted when we are flexible and open minded. If we are open to constructive criticism from our children and willing to change our minds, then our children in turn will tend to be more open to changing their minds too, knowing that they can do so without losing. We need to build on every successful instant of flexible thinking because once no-one fears changing their minds, consent flourishes.

Morality

We can't run close personal relationships on a system of rights and responsibilities and we are unlikely to be able to force ourselves to act in certain ways simply because we are convinced that it is the right thing to do. That said, knowing that consent is moral option is a good basis for motivating change.

Optimism

If we don't think that solutions exist, even in theory, then we are not likely to find them. Consent based living is an optimistic lifestyle; although we make mistakes this does not preclude solutions from being possible and achievable another time.

Practicality

Theoretical solutions are not reassuring if we never find them and constant failure is only likely to leave us wallowing in guilt and self-doubt. Consent based living is not just the best parenting idea; it is also eminently practical. It is a positive mirror image of those vicious cycles in which failure and conflict breed more failure and conflict; finding win-win solutions helps us to find more win-win solutions. Finding consent is helped if we concentrate on consent when we are relaxed and not in the midst of crucial decision making situations; if we think about solutions that have worked well in the past; if we make helpful observations about our children's previous preferences (without them becoming fixed in stone); if we are self aware and know our own preferences and if we develop clear lines of communication in which information can flow without seeming threatening or manipulative. In short, the more we develop a family culture of consent the more practical it becomes.

Living It Now

Whilst the conventional parent assumes that childhood is a preparation for life in the adult world, consent-based parents assume that children's present life is intrinsically valuable. Finding solutions to today's problems is the best way to live not only now, but also for the future. People who are not used to solving problems now, don't suddenly become adept at solving problems because they reach the age of eighteen or thirty or fifty. Moreover, people who are constantly concerned with preparing for the next stage of life often reach the end of their lives wondering why they never did anything they actually wanted to do. This is not to say that we should not have goals and long terms aspirations, but we don't reach those by any other way than by solving today's problems today and living well now to build patterns of living well.

At eleven Cora spent most of her time dabbling with things of interest. She spent a lot of time climbing and playing in the local river. She watched TV, sometimes read novels, played computer games with her brother from time to time and enjoyed drawing, making models and craft activities. Cora had a passion for making jewelry and did lots of beadwork, making her own beads from plastic resins. One day her Dad read an article in the local newspaper about a local silversmith interested in craft apprenticeships and Cora contacts the smith, who, despite being surprised when an eleven year old contacted her, invited Cora to come and spend the day working with her.

Soon Cora was spending lots of time with the silversmith, not only learning practical skills, but discovering an interest in the properties of the metals and the theory behind the craft. She began studying math and chemistry from some books her Dad bought and helped her to work through. By the age of eighteen Cora had a good grounding in chemistry and art, a good understanding of math and a solid apprenticeship behind her with an extensive portfolio of both bead and metal work. Cora got in touch with an art school in Finland where her silversmith mentor did her own apprenticeship and spent three years there and a further year at a British art school before setting up her own business in jewelry design and production at the age of twenty two.

Cora didn't fulfill her goals to become a jewelry designer by being told to apply herself diligently to studies in which she had no interest for the sake of some future benefit. She didn't spend her teenage years preparing to become a twenty something young business woman; feeling miserable and bored and hoping that it would get better one day in the future. Rather she spent her time living well; her experience of problem solving and preference fulfillment in the present simply went on happening. It might have taken many other directions and any one of them would have been fine so long as it fulfilled Cora's preferences.

Throughout this book I've been clear that engaging in consent-based parenting is not magical or always easy. Any parenting method that offers a quick fix will soon come unstuck, but neither is taking time to find consent a chore or a drain. Consent based parenting is not about self surrender, it is about finding solutions that delight everyone, in which everyone can have as much fun and fulfillment as our resourcefulness allows. Living now rather than constantly deferring life for another day assists this enormously.

And So...

There are no rules to live by, but there are ways of thinking that will transform your parenting and have a major positive impact on your relationships and life. Above all, living by consent is about evolving new ways of relating within a win-win environment. Within this environment:

- Limitations are taken seriously; parent, as well as children, can be wrong.
- There is an acknowledgement of everyone's humanity and right to self-determination.
- Parental information, opinions, analysis and experience is valued, but it is not the bottom line or the last word.
- Self interest is valued and nurtured as a good and optimal way of a child making decisions about his or her own life.
- Problem solving is much more important than either giving in to a child's first wish or assuming someone has to lose.
- We can't predict outcomes and futures for our children or describe the product we want them to be, but we can trust that it will be good, even if surprising.
- Solutions are available, even when we don't find them.
- Consent based parenting is not magic, but it is a good and worthwhile journey and the best thing we can do for our children and for ourselves.

In short, finding consent is about using our reason and resourcefulness in a flexible, open minded way within the constraints of our human limitations to build moral, practical and optimistic families in which there are both winning parents and winning children.

Enjoy it.

References

Baughaman, F.A., (2000) *Still Seeking ADHD* American Anthropological Association

Barkley, R., *ADHD* Scientific American online – www.sciam.com

Biddulph, S., (1998) *Raising Boys* HarperCollins

Caruso, D., (1999) Linking entertainment to violence, New York Times

Chilton Pearce, J., (1992) *Magical Child: Rediscovering Nature's Plan for our Children* Harper

Dawkins, R., (1989) *The Selfish Gene* Oxford Paperbacks

Fortune-Wood, J., (2001) *Bound to Be Free* Educational Heretics Press

Fortune-Wood, J., (2000) *Without Boundaries* Educational Heretics Press

Fortune-Wood, J., (2002) *With Consent* Educational Heretics Press

Kohn, A., (1995) *Punished by Rewards* Houghton Mifflin

Liedloff, J., (1989) *The Continuum Concept* Arkana

Pollack, W., *Real Boys, Rescuing Our Sons From The Myths of Boyhood*

Szasz, T.S., (2001) *Chemical Straitjackets for Children* The Foundation for Economic Education

Films:

Tea with Mussolini, a story of civilized disobedience. Zeffireli, F. (1999) Universal Studios

The Matrix (1999) Warner Brothers, Village Roadshow Films (BV) Ltd

Further Reading:

Dawkins, R., (1989) *The Selfish Gene* Oxford Paperbacks

Popper, K., (1995) *The Myth of the Framework* Routledge

Useful Websites:

www.autonomouschild.co.uk
www.amnesty.org
www.choiceineducation.co.uk
www.home-education.org.uk
www.homeeducationresearch.org
www.psychotherapistresources.com
www.sciam.com
www.takingchildrenseriously.com

For the best amongst poetry journals:

Now in large format, perfect bound full colour cover

Celebrating its 50th year of publication.

Envoi show-cases the best in poetry writing from writers in the UK and internationally, as well as carrying poetry features, competitions & essential poetry book reviews. The new *Envoi* website also features poetry & reviews.

For the best of both worlds:
Subscribe to *Envoi* and add an optional Cinnamon Poetry Book club subscription – three of our best new titles at discount prices, **available only to *Envoi* subscribers.**

www.envoipoetry.com

Cinnamon Press Writing Awards:

We run four writing competitions with two deadlines each year – the genres are –
Debut Novel; First Poetry Collection; Novella; Short Story

Deadlines June 30th and November 30th each year.
All entries by post + sae & details - name, address, email, working title, nom de plume.

Novel: 1st prize - £500 + publishing contract. Submit 10,000 words. 5 finalists submit full novel & receive appraisal. Entry - £20 per novel.

Poetry Collection: 1st prize - £100 & publishing contract. Runners up published in anthology. Submit 10 poems up to 40 lines. Three finalists submit further 10 poems, any length. Entry - £16. per collection, includes free copy of winners' anthology.

Novella: 1st prize - £200 + publishing contract (20 – 45,000 words). Submit 10,000 words. Four finalists submit full novella. Entry - £16 per novella.

Short Story: 1st prize - £100 & publication. 10 runners up stories' published in winners' anthology. Length 2,000 – 4,000 words. Entry - £16 per story, includes free copy of winners' anthology.

Entries to: Meirion House, Glan yr afon, Tanygrisiau, Blaenau Ffestiniog, Gwynedd, LL41 3SU

Full details www.cinnamonpress.com